OXFORD WORLD'S CLASSICS

ON CHRISTIAN TEACHING

AUGUSTINE was born in 354, the son of a Christian mother and a pagan father who farmed a few acres at Thagaste (now Souk-Ahras in eastern Algeria). Education at the hands of poor teachers could not hinder his acute mind from acquiring a mastery of classical Latin literature, especially that of Cicero and Virgil. He became a gifted teacher of literature and public speaking successively at Carthage, Rome, and Milan. At Carthage he met a woman by whom he had a son, and with whom he lived faithfully for fifteen years until at Milan she became a fatal block in the path of his secular career. A personal crisis followed. Already in Africa his religious quest took him to Manichee theosophy, then in Italy to scepticism and thence to the Neoplatonic mysticism of Plotinus. In July 386 in a Milan garden he resolved to abandon a secular career and the respectable marriage that would make this possible. Baptized by St Ambrose (387), he buried his widowed mother at Ostia and returned to North Africa (388). Against his will he was forced into ordination in 391 and five years later became bishop at Hippo (modern Annaba) for the remaining thirty-four years of his life. His many writings include the *Confessions* (397)—which gives a detailed account of his mental and spiritual development from infancy to his early thirties—and the massive *City of God*, undertaken after the sack of Rome in 410. *On Christian Teaching* was begun shortly before the *Confessions*, but broken off in midstream and not completed until 427, three years before his death during the Vandal siege of his city (28 August 430).

R. P. H. GREEN was educated in High Wycombe and Oxford, and taught Latin in St Andrews University for many years before becoming Professor of Humanity (Latin) in Glasgow University in 1995. He has published books on Augustine's contemporaries Paulinus of Nola and Ausonius, and has also studied the reception of the classical poets Virgil and Horace in the Middle Ages and Renaissance.

OXFORD WORLD'S CLASSICS

*For almost 100 years Oxford World's Classics have brought
readers closer to the world's great literature. Now with over 700
titles—from the 4,000-year-old myths of Mesopotamia to the
twentieth century's greatest novels—the series makes available
lesser-known as well as celebrated writing.*

*The pocket-sized hardbacks of the early years contained
introductions by Virginia Woolf, T. S. Eliot, Graham Greene,
and other literary figures which enriched the experience of reading.
Today the series is recognized for its fine scholarship and
reliability in texts that span world literature, drama and poetry,
religion, philosophy and politics. Each edition includes perceptive
commentary and essential background information to meet the
changing needs of readers.*

OXFORD WORLD'S CLASSICS

SAINT AUGUSTINE

On Christian Teaching

Translated with an Introduction and Notes by
R. P. H. GREEN

OXFORD
UNIVERSITY PRESS

Oxford University Press, Great Clarendon Street, Oxford OX2 6DP

Oxford New York

Athens Auckland Bangkok Bogotá Buenos Aires Calcutta
Cape Town Chennai Dar es Salaam Delhi Florence Hong Kong Istanbul
Karachi Kuala Lumpur Madrid Melbourne Mexico City Mumbai
Nairobi Paris São Paulo Singapore Taipei Tokyo Toronto Warsaw
and associated companies in Berlin Ibadan

Oxford is a registered trade mark of Oxford University Press

Published in the United States
by Oxford University Press Inc., New York

Translation and editorial matter © R. P. H. Green 1997

First published as a World's Classics paperback 1997
Reissued as an Oxford World's Classics paperback 1999

British Library Cataloguing in Publication Data

Data available

Library of Congress Cataloging in Publication Data

Augustine, Saint, Bishop of Hippo.
[De doctrina Christiana. English]
On Christian teaching / Saint Augustine; translated with an
introduction and notes by R. P. H. Green
(Oxford world's classics)
1. Apologetics—Early works to 1800. 2. Bible—Criticism,
interpretation, etc.—History—Early church, ca. 30–600.
3. Theology—History—Early church, ca. 30–600. I. Title.
II. Series.
BR65.A6552E5 1997 230'.14—dc21 96–40146
ISBN 0–19–283928–4

1 3 5 7 9 10 8 6 4 2

Printed in Great Britain by
Cox & Wyman Ltd.
Reading, Berkshire

Contents

Introduction

Aims and circumstances

When Augustine was ordained presbyter in the African town of Hippo in 391 one of the first things he did was to ask for time off— time to devote himself to intensive study of the Bible. It was just five years since his well-known experience of conversion in the Milanese garden, prompted by a command to pick up and read the scripture. From then on he saw with ever-increasing clarity the need to immerse himself in the 'profundity' and 'riches' of scripture, just as he had dedicated himself (without asking for time off from his teaching duties) to the study of philosophical texts upon his arrival in Milan a few years earlier. One may gauge the scale of the task of study and interpretation which he saw before him from the long list of commentaries and sermons which he eventually left to posterity, with their amazing capacity to synthesize diverse passages of scripture and to elicit, often from obscure if not rebarbative passages, spiritual truths or lessons for himself and others. Yet we must not be so impressed by his later achievements, or by the colourful way in which he often expressed angry feelings about the 'pagan' educational system of his day, as to lose sight of the fact that he had spent half his life as a teacher of secular studies. There is a great deal of the ancient schoolmaster and professor in Augustine: a conviction of the importance of detail, a devotion to what he sees as consistency of interpretation, a reverence for canonical texts as authorities and 'classics' (though classical texts were never seen as sacred in quite the same way as scripture was). Augustine owed a great deal to the system which he criticized so trenchantly.

When he began writing *On Christian Teaching* in the mid-390s he had already embarked on detailed expositions of Genesis, Psalms, and Paul's letters to the Romans and Galatians. Its purpose was to systematize for the benefit of others the observations and principles that had become apparent to him in his study of the Bible, and to enable readers of scripture to be their own interpreters. As he explains in the Preface, his task is parallel to that of a teacher of the alphabet: one of giving fundamental instruction so that others can understand the texts they pick up and read. The word 'teaching' in the title applies primarily to the task of teaching Christianity to oneself and then to others; but it also embraces the teachings of Christianity which may be drawn from scripture. Since for all but a special few (1. 93–4) it is the scriptures which lead Christians to their goal, the work is a guide to the discovery and communication of what is taught in the Bible.

It has often been seen as a manual for preachers (and that is certainly one of its main contributions to Western culture), but Augustine does not forget other kinds of communication, such as debates, books, and letters (4. 102). He nowhere makes it unambiguously clear whether the work is directed solely to the clergy, and in particular bishops, who were involved in preaching, though in 4. 8 he refers to 'those whom we desire to be educated for the good of the church', and in that book as a whole the needs of preachers seem to be uppermost. But it is surely not for all preachers, for he assumes that the communicators have considerable knowledge already, or the means to gain it, and much of his advice would be beyond the comprehension of most preachers of his time.[1] (They might be more reassured by his contention that using the sermons of others was morally above board.) He is writing for 'those with the will and the wit to learn' (Preface, 1), and evidently did not intend to exclude any who could profit. He was certainly always sensitive to the needs of the laity, and ready to help them with problems they encountered in their study of the Bible.

It has also been seen as a manifesto for a specifically Christian culture, not least because of what it says about the value of the learning available outside the church, or, as we would say, pagan or classical culture. There is no doubt that this is a major theme of the work, and one of its major points of interest, but that was not its prime justification. Augustine was not, as used to be thought, constructing a counterpart to the classical culture self-consciously cherished by many pagan Romans of his time. The significance of the title should in fact be found in the various injunctions of the so-called Pastoral Epistles to seek and make use of 'sound teaching' (or 'doctrine', as the Authorized Version has

---

[1] C. Schäublin, '*De doctrina Christiana*: A Classic of Western Culture?', in D. W. H. Arnold and P. Bright (eds.), *De doctrina christiana: A Classic of Western Culture* (Notre Dame, Ind., 1995), 54.

it); these passages are recalled frequently, and in the final sentence of the work he significantly situates his work within that context.

There is probably no need to seek more particular reasons for this 'great and arduous' undertaking than the need to help Christians learn from the Bible. The work is not polemical in any way, although one can detect faint echoes of controversies which loomed large in Augustine's spiritual career. For example, issues such as the apparent acceptance of polygamy in the Old Testament, and the adultery of David (treated at some length in 3. 68–72), formed part of the arsenal of the Manichees or followers of Mani—a popular and dynamic religion on the edges of Christianity whose mission was to proclaim the permanent conflict of Light and Dark, or Good and Evil, and which saw the Old Testament, in contrast to the New, as far too full of the material or evil element to possess spiritual authority. But in fact neither the Manichees themselves nor their distinctive and sometimes colourful tenets are mentioned in this work. Augustine does mention the Donatists—who over the years absorbed so much of his energy as he sought to combat their claim to constitute the true and pure Christian church—when he introduces *The Book of Rules* of Tyconius at the end of Book 3 (92 ff.); but he treats him rather as a maverick than as a heretic, stressing the fact that Tyconius too had wielded his pen against the Donatists. Such reservations as Augustine has he expresses with restraint, and his attitude is generally positive. He is certainly not attacking Tyconius, though it may well have been the appearance of his work some years before that showed him the possibilities of a hermeneutical treatise and encouraged him to provide something better. The suggestion has been made that Augustine wrote his book at the request of his friend the Catholic bishop Aurelius (see *Ep.* 41. 2), but although Aurelius was involved in some way with Augustine's project—at least Augustine asked his opinion several times, evidently without success—it is unlikely that he needed any such prompting.

We do not know precisely when Augustine began the work: perhaps it was in 395.[2] It has been reasonably inferred from 2. 146,

---

[2] For fuller detail, see R. P. H. Green (ed.), *Augustine: De Doctrina Christiana* (Oxford Early Christian Texts; Oxford, 1995), xi–xii.

where he mentions various Christian writers who have exploited pagan education but declares that he is omitting others who are alive, that he wrote this before the death of Ambrose in April 397. But the short chapter about this work in the *Retractations* (a brief review of his writings that he made in the last years of his life) seems also to imply that the work followed after one that he addressed to Ambrose's successor as bishop in Milan, so he seems to have continued past that date. Anyhow, as Augustine himself tells us, it was broken off in midstream, at 3. 78; and what follows was not written until some thirty years later. Various reasons have been suggested for the interruption, including illness (he is known to have been covered by debilitating sores at about that time) and writer's block, brought on by the sheer volume of writing he had undertaken (Augustine was a frenetic writer as well as a voracious reader). There were infinite demands on the time of such a talented and energetic pastor, and further speculation may be unprofitable; but it is just at this time that Augustine began his *Confessions*, which gives an intimate examination of his relationship to God as it developed from infancy, and was perhaps designed to defend his meteoric rise in the Christian church. It is indeed fascinating and instructive to read the works side by side. One can observe how the *Confessions* enacts graphically and personally many of the feelings and insights that *On Christian Teaching* presents in a more abstract way: the ascent (by reasoning and contemplation) to God, the wise and unchangeable one, from the world that is changeable and at best incompletely wise; the difficulties presented to the traveller on this upward path by the weight of sexual inclinations and other habits; the 'pacts' or contracts that for better or worse bind human communities and underlie their distinctive cultures. Most conspicuously, the *Confessions* purports to portray an insider's experience of the educational disciplines which Augustine in Book 2 of *On Christian Teaching* calls burdensome and valueless, and it expresses his contempt for the culture of rhetorical showmanship to which he will briefly but scathingly revert in Book 4.

It is no easier to give a definitive answer to what is perhaps a more pertinent question: why did the completion of this work take so long? Augustine's comment in the *Retractations* rather suggests that he lost sight of it, but it is not likely that he came to consider it unimportant, even if it had to take second place to his sustained attacks on movements which he saw as dangerously schismatic or heretical, or to the completion of vast works such as *City of God* or *On the Trinity*. It is more plausible to attribute the delay to an appreciation that there were issues involved which could not be adequately covered in what he envisaged as a small book. When he eventually resumed work, his approach was rather less discursive than before. He was probably able to make use of some notes he had left (this would explain a certain bittiness in that part of Book 3); these he expanded, before adding a condensed exposition of Tyconius' *Book of Rules*. Book 4 deals with the presentation or communication of what one has learnt, but unless the neat initial division (1. 1) into 'discovery' and presentation is a later addition this important part of the work was part of his plan from the outset. No really convincing differences of substance between the two sections have been detected, though that is not to say that Augustine would have written the same in the late 390s as he eventually did in his old age.

Summary and significance

The short preface that Augustine wrote is probably part of the earlier portion, although this has been disputed; it may therefore be reasonably assumed to present his original conception and justification of the work. He anticipates three kinds of critic: those who cannot understand his advice, those who fail to apply it, and those who consider it unnecessary, because illumination should come directly from God. He directs his attention principally to the third kind, and in refutation appeals to their own experience of learning and the many occasions recorded in scripture when humans were taught through human agency. Augustine then begins his main task by dividing his subject into two parts: the discovery of what must be learnt from scripture, and the presentation of it, or in other words the study of its content and the proclamation of its message. To understand the teaching of scripture we need a knowledge both of 'things' and of 'signs'. The subject of Book 1 will be things *qua* things (for things can be signs, and vice versa). Human beings, themselves a kind of thing, should 'enjoy' some things or cleave to them in love, and 'use' others, relating or subordinating them to the attainment of what they love. The proper object of enjoyment is God, who is universally (but often imperfectly) acknowledged in one way or another.

In order to enjoy him, to behold the light of the divine Trinity continually, the human eye must be purged, and we must travel to God along his chosen way, accepting the carefully designed means of healing offered by the incarnate Christ and taking full advantage of the necessary support provided by his church. Before going further it is interesting to note how this sketch of the Christian life—with the vital exceptions of the roles of Christ and the church—is indebted to concepts prominent in the writings of the philosopher Plotinus. Plotinus, who flourished a century or so before Augustine, was the outstanding member of a philosophical movement devoted to the study of Plato; Augustine and others called them Platonists but modern scholars refer to them as Neoplatonists, in recognition of their impressively distinctive philosophical system. (At the end of Book 2 Augustine admits their value to the Christian, and indeed it used to be said, with the exaggeration that often accompanies an important insight, that he had been converted to Neoplatonism and not Christianity.) The remainder of the book is devoted to giving answers to various problems that arise from this understanding of love in terms of use and enjoyment. Should humans use each other or enjoy each other? In what way should they love themselves? Which of the things to be used should be loved? Is it possible to hate oneself? Can all people be loved equally in practice? Does the commandment to love one's neighbour apply to the angels? Does God, in loving us, enjoy us or use us? The importance of these careful discussions is that the two commandments to love God and to love our neighbour as ourselves are 'the fulfilment and end of the law', and so our interpretations of scripture—which cannot lie, although we may be misled as we try to interpret it—should be ones which serve to build up this love. Its importance in the wider context of Augustine's general thinking on love is rather less; it has been shown that the distinctive analysis of love in terms of enjoyment and use was never repeated by Augustine. In retrospect the book must be regarded as experimental and inconclusive.[3] None the less it remains a careful and sensitive discussion of various problems in this area of Biblical ethics.

[3] O. O'Donovan, *The Problem of Self-Love in St. Augustine* (New Haven, 1980), 26.

In Book 2 Augustine takes up the treatment of signs *qua* signs. The apparently simple analysis with which the book begins has in fact been described as the first piece of work to deserve the name of semiotics (though the degree of its originality *vis-à-vis* classical philosophy has been much debated). Certainly this aspect has contributed greatly to modern interest in this work and others in which his sign-theory is applied. Attention has also been drawn to the way in which his view of signs, as developed in Books 2 and 3, enables him to explore the boundaries and interrelations of communities or subcultures which share particular symbolic systems.[4] Of particular note in the opening chapters are Augustine's definition of a sign, his distinction between 'natural' and 'given' signs, and the part played in the latter by intention or will. Words are a particular kind of sign, and one which is particularly problematic in the Bible not only because of the diversity of languages but also because God in his wisdom has provided a level of difficulty appropriate to the needs of the human mind. Problems arise either from unknown signs or from ambiguous ones, and both these kinds of signs may be either literal or metaphorical (figurative). Book 2 will deal with literal signs, beginning with the former category. What do foreign words in scripture, or imperfectly translated Latin ones, really mean? The serious student, equipped with Christian virtues as well as a wide knowledge of the canonical scriptures (here Augustine sets out the canon best known to him), must be prepared to learn the relevant languages or at least to consult experts, and to examine the original versions and the various available translations. Sometimes hyperliteral and stilted translations have more to offer than those written in good Latin. In order to understand metaphorical signs that may be unknown, one also needs a knowledge of the various things referred to in scripture. It may, for example, take analogies from the natural world—how exactly do we set about being as wise as serpents?—or express its meaning in terms of number and music. So the study of music for this purpose is quite proper; the pagan fancies associated with the Muses should not lead to a contempt of music itself. At this point the investigation might

---

[4] See R. A. Markus, 'Signs, Communication and Communities in Augustine's *De doctrina Christiana*', in Arnold and Bright, *De doctrina christiana*, 97–108.

have degenerated into a list of bits and pieces of 'general knowledge' (or abstruse knowledge, as general knowledge often is), had not Augustine changed tack and put the investigation on a systematic footing. In fact he makes a classification of the arts and sciences which is of major importance. The various arts and sciences are either human institutions or divine ones which humans have observed and developed. Of human institutions some are superstitious, like astrology, and their significance is due to pacts or contracts with demons; these must be strenuously avoided. Of those that are not superstitious, some are superfluous and self-indulgent, like the study of representational art, and therefore a dangerous waste of time for the Christian, but others are necessary to life, like a knowledge of weights and measures, the alphabet, or shorthand. The latter are not to be avoided, but used with due care, as may be necessary. Divinely instituted disciplines include history (which narrates, or perhaps to Augustine *is* the past, which cannot be changed), various sciences such as medicine and astronomy (though the borderline with superstition is a difficult one to locate), practical arts such as joinery and navigation, and various arts 'involving the mind', among which logic and rhetoric are pre-eminent. Philosophy is added, almost (it seems) as an afterthought, perhaps in recognition of Augustine's personal experience. All these must be studied in moderation and with a humble acknowledgement that knowledge puffs up but love builds up, and that the treasures of pagan books are tiny when compared with those of scripture. This last analogy—comparing the wealth of scripture with that of King Solomon—has been rather overshadowed by the more famous one of 'spoiling the Egyptians', echoed in the *Confessions* and by many later writers. Like the Hebrews leaving Egypt, Christians who leave pagan society should take with them those riches which they can legitimately use. In Augustine's case, these cultural riches consisted predominantly of philosophy (he was very aware of his Platonist heritage, but probably less so of what he owed to the Stoics through Cicero and other channels), and rhetoric: Book 4 shows the extent of what he owed to classical rhetorical theory, and the whole treatise, on almost every page, the way in which he put his experience of learning and teaching rhetoric to practical use.

Augustine's analysis of the traditional curriculum, perhaps the most systematic appraisal of it that was made in antiquity, is an interesting mixture of the practical and the theoretical. On the one hand he recommends the compilation, or wider distribution, of manuals on such things as Hebrew names or botanical terms found in the Bible, as if he is thinking of the needs of Christians already educated; on the other, he seems to be trying to work out *ab initio* what kinds of knowledge and expertise it might be useful for Christian children to acquire. Yet it is not exhaustive: it is notable that he omits all mention of *grammatice*, which was studied in the school curriculum for several years before rhetoric and included not only systematic formal grammar but also careful study of the canonical Latin poets. It is clear, especially if the *Confessions* is taken into account, that Augustine had reservations both about grammar as conventionally taught and about classical poetry; but he would not have hesitated to place the discipline among those divinely instituted. Language, and so grammar, was part of the divine creation, and poetry is found in the Bible, as Augustine recognizes. He himself is not immune to the power of poetry, as is shown by his discussion of imagery from the Song of Songs (2. 11–13), and by the occasional reminiscences in his writing of phrases from the classical poets Virgil, Lucan, and Persius.

Having dealt with 'unknown' or unfamiliar signs in Book 2, Augustine turns to 'ambiguous' ones in Book 3. Literal words or expressions may cause difficulty if there are uncertainties of punctuation and pronunciation, so due attention must be given to these. Figurative expressions require even more; to take literally what has a spiritual significance is a mark of slavery, conspicuous in the Old Testament Jews, though less serious there than in pagan society with its much worse confusion of sign and thing. But there is an opposite danger, that of taking as figurative what should be taken literally; a danger aggravated by the tendency of people to judge past ages according to their own familiar standards and not by the ethical principles of the Bible, which are the nourishing of love and the overcoming of lust. To help in deciding whether an expression is literal or figurative Augustine presents various guidelines. Cruel words in the mouth of God or a saint will refer literally to the destruction of lust; wicked words or deeds issuing from one whose sanctity is commended will be figurative. Such a person should not be censured, especially by those who are ignorant of the conditions prevailing in former times. An expression which forbids wickedness or enjoins kindness is not figurative; but one which apparently does enjoin wickedness (drinking a man's blood, for example) or forbid kindness will be. One must beware of taking as figurative certain commands (such as castrating oneself or giving a daughter in marriage) which scripture addresses exclusively to particular categories of people, or the non-condemnatory description of practices such as polygamy which though now unacceptable were not wrong in former days. It is a sign of depravity to censure such things, and even worse to do them.

Augustine had carefully summed up and apparently completed this section to his satisfaction before he broke off, but there is much that is unclear. Later writers in general found this the least rewarding of the four books. Are we dealing exclusively with moral precepts, and not with descriptive phrases such as 'the anger of God' and 'crucifying the flesh', which he mentions once (3. 40) in a very brief parenthesis? How do we distinguish between a moral absolute and a practice or precept justified by particular circumstances? If adultery may be justified in a society in the Old Testament, what about cruelty? How exactly may a passage be both literal and figurative, as he says (in 3. 73) that everything, or nearly everything, in the Old Testament is? When we examine a passage from all angles in order to find the true meaning (3. 76) what do we actually do, and what procedures are legitimate?

The rest of the book offers assistance in working out what a particular figurative word or expression means. A particular word will not always have the same figurative sense. Easy passages should be used to illustrate the obscure. If a meaning is reached which was not intended by the human author of scripture, it is not necessarily wrong. Scripture in fact—this is addressed to the literati—contains innumerable tropes. At this point Augustine brings in the seven rules of Tyconius, the Donatist exegete, in which he clearly found much of value, though less than Tyconius had claimed for them. He rejects the third ('On the promises and the Law', in Tyconius' formulation), as being a doctrinal problem rather than a rule of interpretation, but summarizes the other six, using Tyconius' shorter examples to show how they should be applied. The fourth ('On species and genus') he seems to misunderstand when interpreting it of whole and part rather than type and antitype, and there is controversy about his understanding of the sixth ('On Recapitulation'), where Tyconius himself is puzzlingly brief. Augustine argues that these rules are essentially figurative, because 'they cause one thing to be understood through another', but one might better describe them as revealing latent modes of transition from one topic to another: from the head to the body (as in the first, referring to Christ, and the seventh, referring to the devil), or from the bad to the good (as in the second, which Augustine would have rather called 'On the mixed church').

In Book 4, after announcing the second part of his project, on presentation, and warning his readers not to expect a rhetorical treatise of the traditional kind, Augustine issues a rousing appeal to Christians not to shrink from using rhetoric in defence of the faith: this is neutral ground, which Christian speakers must occupy. They do not need a traditional education, with its surfeit of rules, but can acquire eloquence much more quickly by listening to eloquent Christians and imitating them; there is no lack of Christian speakers and writers who show the necessary combination of eloquence and wisdom. For the speaker who does not succeed in acquiring eloquence, close adherence to the words of scripture is an acceptable option. Augustine then raises the question whether the scriptures are eloquent as well as wise, and maintains that they do have their own special kind of eloquence, which he proceeds to illustrate by analysing (principally in terms of sentence structure) a passage from Paul and one from Amos. The Christian speaker is warned not to imitate scripture in those passages where it has been made deliberately obscure, because in addressing a popular audience the need for intelligibility is paramount. In the interests of his listeners a speaker may even need to choose colloquial usages that offend the ears of the educated. A discussion of the importance of holding an audience's attention leads Augustine to introduce and explain the Ciceronian doctrine of the orator's three aims—to teach, to delight, and to move—which he later rephrases as 'to be listened to with understanding, with pleasure, and with obedience' (4. 87). With due allowance for the danger of overdoing the entertainment, the

Christian speaker should make these aims his own. They are then combined with another Ciceronian triad—the eloquent speaker will speak of small things in the restrained style, moderate things in the mixed style, and important things in the grand style—but this is found to be inappropriate in the ecclesiastical context, where there are no matters of minor importance. Augustine then illustrates the three styles by means of excerpts from the writings of Paul, Cyprian, and Ambrose, and shows how they reflect different aims. But within an address the three styles may, indeed must, be combined, in whatever ways context or contrast may demand. For Augustine, unlike other orators, the aim of giving pleasure is the least important of the three, and he also stresses that while using any one style the speaker must be aware of all three aims. The book ends by emphasizing requirements of a specifically Christian nature: the integrity of the speaker's life, a concern with the truth rather than with wrangling, and, whether the speaker is about to deliver his own sermon or one composed by someone else (as he may quite legitimately do), the need to pray for words that will communicate effectively.

Book 4, with its wealth of observation both general and particular, has probably been the most influential part of *On Christian Teaching*. The Ciceronian framework is clear, and numerous details show how well Augustine knew the relevant writings. (There are various, less obvious borrowings from Cicero in other books too.) But a catalogue of his allusions would be a poor guide. Augustine is far from accepting Ciceronian theory unreservedly. Just as he heavily adapted the rhetorical notion of 'discovery' when outlining his programme, so here he treats Cicero as he sees fit. Indeed, a modern reader might well ask why he relies so much on Cicero in the first place. The answer is not that Augustine is eager to show his learning or the effectiveness with which he can deconstruct a pagan classic—as may be the case in other works— but that Cicero was the embodiment, imperfect but by far the best available, of the divinely instituted truths of rhetoric. Some of what Cicero said is as immovable for Augustine as the truths of logic or mathematics; some is open to modification. Augustine is not toying with his classical predecessor or showing an exaggerated deference but carefully and seriously attempting to sift his advice—a good example of the careful examination of traditional disciplines recommended in Book 2. His discriminating blend of classical and Christian precept contains much that is valuable. To the ordinary preacher he has given reassurance of the eloquence of the Bible, the power of prayer, and the reasonableness of using borrowed material, as well as salutary instruction on the importance of keeping basic goals in view and appreciating the needs of an audience. To the educated Christian he has provided, on top of this, a delineation of what is permanently useful in the art of rhetoric, a strong legitimation of its use, and a clear demonstration of its presence both in the scriptures and in the Church Fathers. That Augustine should not only explicitly accept, but also warmly embrace, rhetoric in this way is an important landmark in the history of Christianity; but given that Christians had not in fact been slow to do this, and could perhaps hardly have done otherwise, the book's most important long-term effect may have been not so much to convince Christians of the legitimacy of rhetoric as to reassure them of the acceptability of scriptural style in a world still delighted by the influence of its classical heritage.

Reception and influence

What makes a classic? Some works take their place on the shelf immediately, and stay there, perhaps unmoved for centuries. Some earn the title by the grandeur of their conception or the thoroughness with which they pursue it, or both: such is the *City of God*. Some works, even if by some misfortune they were to be lost or forgotten, would reconstitute themselves as classics in any reasonably sympathetic age: such is the *Confessions*. For *On Christian Teaching*, admittedly the least known of Augustine's three major works which deal in some way with the relation of Christianity to classical culture, we may immediately assert a claim on two general grounds (or three, if the organizing of a conference solely devoted to it is a good criterion[5]). First, the number of manuscripts known to have existed in the Carolingian Renaissance (a good vantage point, since under the inspiration of Charlemagne and his scholars, book production in western

---

[5] Held in the University of Notre Dame, 4–7 April 1991. Its two-volume proceedings, especially the second volume, have contributed a great deal to the following pages.

Europe had begun again in earnest), when its diffusion was surpassed among works of Augustine only by the *City of God*. It was considered well worth the cost and effort of transcribing, and it was widely available to learned readers. Secondly, one can assemble an impressive list of leading medieval and Renaissance authorities who not only knew the work—it is not just our footnote-happy age that seeks to impress through citations—but read and used it, including Cassiodorus, Raban Maur, Abelard, Thomas Aquinas, Roger Bacon, and Erasmus. In the fifth century there is no clear evidence of its use or popularity, but this is not unexpected. It is often not possible to trace the fortunes of an ancient work immediately after its publication, and in this case other circumstances may have contributed to the silence. By the time of his death Augustine had written so much on the Bible, and gained such authority, that the task of independent enquiry may have seemed daunting or unnecessary to less talented Christians. The conditions of the time, with the barbarian Vandals seizing the capital of Roman Africa within a year of his death, and the situation in other areas of the Latin-speaking West little better, did not encourage study.

If Augustine in Book 4 was seeking to vindicate the eloquence of scripture by showing how much it shared with traditional forms of rhetoric, some later interpreters, in a world where scriptural thought and expression rapidly became the norm, exploited this common ground to the advantage of the increasingly threatened pagan classics. This is clear in the work of the senator Cassiodorus, who, in the sixth century, compiled for his monks in Vivarium a syllabus of works concerned with divine and human learning (his *Institutiones*). He is the first of many to use the rallying cry of 'spoiling the Egyptians' to validate the study of pagan classics. Other quotations made by Cassiodorus—who tends to excerpt rather than comment—include advice on how to study scripture. A less memorable testimony is that of the abbot Eugippius who, also in the sixth century, compiled a large but unambitious collection of more than three hundred sayings of Augustine. In the seventh century the Spanish bishop Isidore did likewise in his so-called *Etymologies*, albeit with a wider aim and a much wider range of sources than either of the aforementioned. Evidence of close engagement with our work is as yet non-existent.

The popularity of the work in the Carolingian Renaissance has already been mentioned; the travels of manuscripts can be mapped, and the palace library is known to have had a copy. Books have other uses besides being read or keeping scribes quiet; Angilbert of Corbie sent a copy as a gift to Charlemagne's successor Louis the Pious. The tradition of mere compilation continued, with Raban Maur of Fulda copying several passages in his treatise *On the Instruction of Clerics*, but the work is used more imaginatively, and in a way which foreshadows later development, in a rhetorical treatise presented to Adalram of Salzburg in the mid-ninth century. Its anonymous writer, though following the master closely in many respects, was not afraid to delete the 'mixed' style (here indeed he might be taking his lead from Augustine), vary the terminology, and make other changes.[6]

In the so-called twelfth-century Renaissance *On Christian Teaching* does not appear particularly prominent, even in the Biblical exegetes of the school of St Victor. There is, however, an outstanding exception in Peter Abelard, one of the most lively minds of his age, to whom the work clearly appealed. He quotes Book 4 prominently in the introduction to his famous *Yes and No*, in which he boldly set out apparently conflicting judgements from the Church Fathers on various theological issues. A motif from 1. 27 (God, like a good doctor, applies bandages of an appropriate kind to our wounds) is used in one of his hymns to the Paraclete. Most typical of all, perhaps, he claims Augustine's authority for the importance he gives to logic in his *Introduction to Theology*, where he attempts to use human logic as a bait to lead men and women to theological truth. For Abelard logic (which Augustine had said runs through scripture like a nervous system through the human body) was the treasure of the Egyptians; for Thomas Aquinas in the following century it was philosophy in general. A recent article has shown very carefully how Thomas used *On Christian Teaching* in his great *Summa* and in other work, quoting him on such matters as the nature of scriptural language (how clear passages exist to explain the obscure) and the way to distinguish between literal and figurative expressions. Other scholastics of the time, such as Henry of Ghent, draw copiously from

---

[6] K. Förstner, *Mittellateinisches Jahrbuch*, 4 (1967), 61–7.

On Christian Teaching. The work's contribution to thirteenth-century treatments of theology is a respected and prominent one.[7]

Some two centuries later *On Christian Teaching* was an early beneficiary of printing, and indeed the first book of Augustine to be so honoured. Its fourth book (in fact that was all that emerged at this stage) was seen as a potential best-seller for the aspiring preacher, and it evidently was one for a few years. The work seems to have made little stir among Italian humanists, who for all their interest in teaching and rhetoric quote it but rarely.[8] Erasmus, however, was an enthusiast, not surprisingly given his particular interest in the Christian Fathers who adapted the Greco-Roman classics; one work that shows this influence is his popular *Enchiridion*.[9] George Buchanan, the Scottish humanist influenced by the Erasmian atmosphere in early sixteenth-century Paris, quoted Augustine's sign-theory to defend his position on the Eucharist when arraigned before the Spanish Inquisition. But Augustine was the preserve of no single religious party: after the Council of Trent we find a number of homiletic works, modelled on Book 4, produced under the aegis of Charles Borromeo in Milan.

To pursue the fortunes of Augustine himself, let alone a particular work, through the religious and philosophical disputes and debates of the following centuries would be an arduous and intricate task. *On Christian Teaching* duly took its place in the drab but invaluable *opera omnia* editions of the seventeenth and nineteenth centuries, and was slow to benefit from the subsequent age of critical monograph and translation. One sometimes feels that earlier in the present century the work was quoted (especially in literary contexts) rather than studied, but the present generation has seen a total reversal, in the fortunes of this particular work as in approaches to Augustine himself. Today's Augustine remains a man of intense spirituality and striking insight, but he is also a

[7] J. Wawrykow, 'Reflections on the Place of the *De doctrina christiana* in High Scholastic Discussions of Theology', in E. D. English (ed.), *Reading and Wisdom: The De doctrina christiana of Augustine in the Middle Ages* (Notre Dame, Ind., 1995), 99–125.

[8] J. Monfasani, 'The *De doctrina Christiana* and Renaissance Rhetoric', in English, *Reading and Wisdom*, 172–88.

[9] C. Bène, *Erasme et St Augustin* (Geneva, 1969), 183–6 and 433–48.

multi-dimensional human being; a man subject to great personal and professional pressures, struggling to make sense of his past and striving towards the future, and taking thought for his own flock and the whole church while seeking to do justice to his own great mind. Not the least attraction of *On Christian Teaching* is that this is the Augustine whom we see at work in it.

Note on the Text

The text used for this translation is the one presented in my edition in the Oxford Early Christian Texts series. For this work we have not only hundreds of medieval and later manuscripts but a manuscript unusually close to Augustine in time, which some have argued was dictated or even written by Augustine himself. But neither circumstance gives a cast-iron guarantee that the text is free of serious copying mistakes; early manuscripts are no less prone to such error than later ones, and once a mistake is made it is much more likely that it will be perpetuated by subsequent copying than corrected. So it should not be assumed that the text of this treatise is word-perfect; there are a few places where the argument is uncertain, and rather more where the Latin critic is not yet content.

In the course of time the text has acquired no fewer than three systems of numbering its paragraphs or sections. None of them is notably more valuable than the others as a guide to the argument, and so I have adopted for marginal references and for cross-referencing purposes the system which divides the text into the smallest sections, and is thus the most efficient. The other systems, which are older and more often used, appear as running heads.

Note on Biblical references. References to Psalms and the books generally known as 1 and 2 Samuel are provided in dual form. In the case of Psalms this is because there are two systems of numbering, one being that of the Hebrew text, which is followed by most available English versions, the other being that of the Greek and Latin translations. From Psalm 10 to Psalm 148 the Latin numbering known to Augustine is one less than that in Hebrew and English texts; Psalms 9 and 10 were a single Psalm for Augustine, as were Psalms 114 and 115, while our Psalms 116 and 147 were each two. It is therefore the second of the two references that is likely to be the one familiar to English readers. The books which Augustine knew as 3 and 4 Kings are generally known today as 1 and 2 Kings, and his 1 and 2 Kings as 1 and 2 Samuel; again the second of the references given is likely to be the familiar one.

Select Bibliography

Edition and Translation

Green, R. P. H., *Augustine: De Doctrina Christiana* (Oxford Early Christian Texts; Oxford, 1995).

Biography of Augustine

Brown, P., *Augustine of Hippo: A Biography* (London, 1967).
Chadwick, H., *Augustine* (Oxford, 1986).
van der Meer, F., *Augustine the Bishop* (London, 1961).

Background

Bonnardière, A.-M. (ed.), *Saint Augustin et la Bible*, iii (Bible de Tous les Temps; Paris, 1986).
Hagendahl, H., *Augustine and the Latin Classics*, 2 vols. (Gothenburg, 1967).
Kaster, R. A., *Guardians of Language: The Grammarian and Society in Late Antiquity* (Berkeley, 1988).
Marrou, H.-I., *Saint Augustin et la fin de la culture antique* (Paris, 1938).

Criticism

Arnold, D. W. H., and Bright, P. (eds.), *De doctrina christiana: A Classic of Western Culture* (Notre Dame, Ind., 1995).
Kirwan, C., *Augustine* (London, 1989).
Markus, R. A. (ed.), *Collected Essays on Augustine* (New York, 1972).
O'Donovan, O., *The Problem of Self-Love in St. Augustine* (New Haven, 1980).

Other Works

Chadwick, H. (ed.), *Saint Augustine: Confessions* (Oxford, 1991).
Clark, G., *Augustine: The Confessions* (Cambridge, 1993).

Influence

English, E. D. (ed.), *Reading and Wisdom: The De doctrina christiana of Augustine in the Middle Ages* (Notre Dame, Ind., 1995).

Dates

354 — Augustine born at Thagaste in Numidia
366–9 — At school in Madauros
370 — Goes to Carthage
373–5 — Teaches at Thagaste; a 'hearer' of the Manichees
376 — Teaches at Carthage
383 — Goes to Rome
384 — Appointed professor of rhetoric at Milan, where he also reads 'Platonic books' and meets Ambrose
386 — Converted; retreats to Cassiciacum
387 — Baptized at Milan
391 — Ordained at Hippo Regius
395? — Begins *On Christian Teaching*
395/6 — Becomes bishop of Hippo
397? — Breaks off *On Christian Teaching*
397 — Writes *Confessions*
413–26 — Composes *City of God*
426/7 — Completes *On Christian Teaching*
430 — Death at Hippo

On Christian Teaching

PREFACE

There are certain rules for interpreting the scriptures which, 1
as I am well aware, can usefully be passed on to those with an
appetite for such study to enable them to progress not just by
reading the work of others who have illuminated the obscurities of divine literature, but also by finding illumination themselves.* It is my intention to communicate these rules to those
with the will and the wit to learn, if my Lord and God does not
withhold from me, as I write, the thoughts which he regularly
supplies as I reflect on these matters. But before I begin it 2
seems necessary for me to reply to those who are likely to
criticize this undertaking, or who would be minded to do so if
not placated in advance. If, even after this, there are criticisms
from certain people, at least they will not succeed in mislead-
ing others or in diverting them from this valuable study into
the idleness of ignorance, as they might have done had they not
found them forearmed and forewarned.

Some people will criticize this work of mine because they have 3
failed to understand the rules that I am about to give. Others,
wishing to make use of what they have understood, will try to
interpret the divine scriptures by means of these rules but will
be unable to find illumination or to explain what they want to
explain, and will therefore consider my efforts futile. Because
they themselves get no help from this work, they will conclude
that nobody can. A third class of critic* consists of those who 4
either interpret the divine scriptures quite correctly or think
they do. Because they see, or at least believe, that they have
gained their ability to expound the holy books without
recourse to any rules of the kind that I have now undertaken to
give, they will clamour that these rules are not needed by anybody, and that all worthwhile illumination of the difficulties of
these texts can come by a special gift of God.

To all these critics I have a brief reply. I say to those who fail 5
to understand what I write that it is not my fault that they do
not understand. Suppose they wanted to see the new moon, or
the old one, or a star that was very faint, and I pointed it out

with my finger but their eyesight was too weak to see even my finger—surely it would be wrong for them to be annoyed with
6 me for that reason? As for those who manage to learn and assimilate these rules but are still unable to see into the obscure passages of the divine scriptures, they should consider themselves as capable of seeing my finger but not the stars to which it points. Both types of objector should stop blaming me and pray for insight to be given them by God. Although I can move a part of my body so as to point to something, I cannot improve their eyesight to make them see even my pointing finger, let alone what I want to point out.

7   Now for those who exult in their divine gift and boast that they understand and interpret the sacred books without rules of the kind that I now plan to give, and so consider superfluous what I have chosen to say. Their excitement must be restrained by the recollection that although they have a perfect right to rejoice in their great gift from God they nevertheless learned
8 even the alphabet with human help. Yet that would be no good reason for them to feel humiliated by the holy and perfect Egyptian monk Anthony,* who, though lacking any knowledge of the alphabet, is reported to have memorized the divine scriptures by listening to them being read, and to have understood them by thoughtful meditation; or indeed by the barbarian Christian slave,* who (as we have recently been told by serious and trustworthy people) achieved a complete knowledge of the alphabet itself, without any human instruction, by praying for it to be revealed, and who after three days' prayer managed to read through a book that was offered to him, to the
9 utter amazement of those present. But if anyone thinks these reports untrue, I will not make an issue of it. My argument is with Christians who congratulate themselves on a knowledge of the holy scriptures gained without any human guidance and who—if their claim is valid—thus enjoy a real and substantial blessing. But they must admit that each one of us learnt our native language by habitually hearing it spoken from the very beginnings of childhood, and acquired others—Greek, Hebrew, or whatever—either by hearing them in the same way
10 or by learning them from a human teacher. So should we now (I ask you!*) warn all our brethren not to teach these things to

their small children, on the grounds that the apostles spoke in the languages of all peoples after being inspired in a single moment by the coming of the Holy Spirit [Acts 2: 1–4]? Or should we warn those to whom such things do not happen to stop thinking of themselves as Christians and start doubting that they have received the Holy Spirit? No, they should learn, without any pride, what has to be learned from a human teacher; and those responsible for teaching others should pass on, without pride or jealousy, the knowledge they have received. Let us not tempt the one in whom we have placed our trust, or we may be deceived by the enemy's cunning and perversity and become unwilling even to go to church to hear and learn the gospel, or to read the Biblical text or listen to it being read and preached, preferring to wait until 'we are caught up into the third heaven, whether in the body or out of the body' (in the words of the apostle) [2 Cor. 12: 2–4], and there hear 'words that cannot be expressed, which a human being may not utter' or see the Lord Jesus Christ in person and hear the gospel from him rather than from men.

Let us beware of such arrogant and dangerous temptations, and rather reflect that the apostle Paul, no less, though cast to the ground and then enlightened by a divine voice from heaven, was sent to a human being to receive the sacrament of baptism and be joined to the church [Acts 9: 3–8]. And Cornelius the centurion, although an angel announced to him that his prayers had been heard and his acts of charity remembered, was nevertheless put under the tuition of Peter not only to receive the sacrament but also to learn what should be the objects of his faith, hope, and love.* All this could certainly have been done through an angel, but the human condition would be wretched indeed if God appeared unwilling to minister his word to human beings through human agency. It has been said, 'For God's temple is holy, and that temple you are' [1 Cor. 3: 17]: how could that be true if God did not make divine utterances from his human temple but broadcast direct from heaven or through angels the learning that he wished to be passed on to mankind? Moreover, there would be no way for love, which ties people together in the bonds of unity, to make souls overflow and as it were intermingle with each other, if

14 human beings learned nothing from other humans. And, to be sure, the eunuch who was reading the prophet Isaiah [Acts 8: 26–35] but could not understand him was not sent by an angel to the apostle; nor was the passage that he could not understand explained to him by an angel or divinely revealed within his mind without human assistance. In fact Philip, who knew the prophet Isaiah, was sent to him by divine prompting and sat with him, revealing in human words and human language
15 the passage of scripture that he had found impenetrable. Is it not true that God spoke with Moses, and yet Moses accepted advice about guiding and governing such a great people from his father-in-law, a man actually of another race, with an abundance of foresight and an absence of pride [Exod. 18]? He was well aware that true advice, from whatever mind it came, should be ascribed not to man but to the unchangeable God who is the truth.

16 Finally, anyone who boasts that without having been taught any rules he can understand the difficult passages in the scriptures, by virtue of a divine gift, does well to believe—for it is quite true—that this ability does not somehow originate within the human mind but is given by God: in this way he seeks God's glory, not his own. But if he reads and understands without any human expositor, why does he then aspire to expound it to others and not simply refer them to God so that they too may understand it by God's inner teaching rather than
17 through a human intermediary? Because, of course, he is afraid of being told by his master, 'Wicked servant, you should have put my money on deposit' [Matt. 25: 26–7]. Just as these interpreters reveal to others, whether in speech or in writing, what they learn, so do I: and if I reveal not only what I understand but also the rules to be observed in the process of understanding it, I should surely not incur their criticism. Yet nobody should regard anything as his own, except perhaps a lie.* For all truth comes from the one who says, 'I am the truth' [John 14: 6]. What do we possess that we have not received from another? And if we have received it from another, why give ourselves airs, as if we had not received it [1 Cor. 4: 7]?
18 The teacher who reads out a text to listening students simply articulates what he recognizes; but the teacher who teaches

the actual alphabet has the intention of enabling others to read too. Both are instilling knowledge they have received. The teacher who expounds what he understands in the scriptures expounds it to his listeners, like the reader of a text articulating the letters which he recognizes; whereas the teacher who teaches how to understand scripture is like the teacher of the alphabet, one who teaches how to read. So the person who knows how to read, on finding a book, does not require another reader to tell him what is written in it; and in the same way the person who has assimilated the rules that I am trying to teach, when he finds a difficulty in the text, will not need another interpreter to reveal what is obscure, because he comprehends certain rules (the equivalent of letters in this analogy). By following up various clues he can unerringly arrive at the hidden meaning for himself or at least avoid falling into incongruous misconceptions.

So although it may be clear enough in the book itself that it would be wrong for anyone to speak out against this work of practical utility, I hope that these opening words will be seen to provide an adequate reply to any who object. Such is the introduction that suggested itself to me as I set out along the road that I want to follow in this book.

BOOK ONE

1 There are two things on which all interpretation of scripture depends: the process of discovering what we need to learn, and the process of presenting what we have learnt. I shall discuss the process of discovery* first, and then that of presentation. This is a great and arduous burden,* one difficult to sustain and also, I fear, a rash one to undertake; or so it would be if I were trusting in my own resources. But since in fact my hope of completing the work is based on God, from whom I already have much relevant material through meditation, I have no need to worry that he will fail to supply the remainder when

2 I begin to share what has been given to me. For all the things which do not give out when given away are not properly possessed when they are possessed but not given away. God says, 'the man who has will be given more' [Matt. 13: 12]. He will give to those who have: this means that for those who make generous use of what they have received he will supplement and increase what he has given. One person had five loaves, and another had seven before the loaves began to be distributed to the hungry, but once the distribution had begun, they managed to fill baskets and hampers even after satisfying so many

3 thousands of people [Matt. 14: 17–21; 15: 34–8]. So just like the bread, which increased as it was broken, the material which God has already supplied to me for starting this work will be multiplied, through his own provision, when discussion of it begins. So in this act of service I will not only experience no shortage of material, but in fact enjoy an astonishing abundance of it.

4 All teaching is teaching of either things or signs, but things are learnt through signs. What I now call things in the strict sense are things such as logs, stones, sheep, and so on, which are not employed to signify something; but I do not include the log which we read that Moses threw into the bitter waters to make them lose their bitter taste [Exod. 15: 25], or the stone which Jacob placed under his head [Gen. 28: 11], or the sheep which Abraham sacrificed in place of his son [Gen. 22: 13].

These are things, but they are at the same time signs of other things. There are other signs whose whole function consists in signifying.* Words, for example: nobody uses words except in order to signify something. From this it may be understood what I mean by signs: those things which are employed to signify something. So every sign is also a thing, since what is not a thing does not exist. But it is not true that every thing is also a sign. Therefore in my distinction of things and signs, when I speak of things, I shall speak of them in such a way that even if some of them can be employed to signify they do not impair the arrangement by which I will treat things first and signs later. And we must be careful to remember that what is under consideration at this stage is the fact that things exist, not that they signify something else besides themselves.

There are some things which are to be enjoyed, some which are to be used, and some whose function is both to enjoy and use. Those which are to be enjoyed make us happy; those which are to be used assist us and give us a boost, so to speak, as we press on towards our happiness, so that we may reach and hold fast to the things which make us happy. And we, placed as we are among things of both kinds, both enjoy and use them; but if we choose to enjoy things that are to be used, our advance is impeded and sometimes even diverted, and we are held back, or even put off, from attaining things which are to be enjoyed, because we are hamstrung by our love of lower things.

To enjoy something is to hold fast to it in love for its own sake. To use something is to apply whatever it may be to the purpose of obtaining what you love—if indeed it is something that ought to be loved. (The improper use of something should be termed abuse.) Suppose we were travellers who could live happily only in our homeland, and because our absence made us unhappy we wished to put an end to our misery and return there: we would need transport by land or sea which we could use to travel to our homeland, the object of our enjoyment. But if we were fascinated by the delights of the journey and the actual travelling, we would be perversely enjoying things that we should be using; and we would be reluctant to finish our journey quickly, being ensnared in the wrong kind of pleasure and estranged* from the homeland whose pleasures could

9 make us happy. So in this mortal life we are like travellers away from our Lord [2 Cor. 5: 6]: if we wish to return to the homeland where we can be happy we must use this world [cf. 1 Cor. 7: 31], not enjoy it, in order to discern 'the invisible attributes of God, which are understood through what has been made' [Rom. 1: 20] or, in other words, to derive eternal and spiritual value from corporeal and temporal things.

10   The things which are to be enjoyed, then, are the Father and the Son and the Holy Spirit, and the Trinity that consists of them, which is a kind of single, supreme thing, shared by all who enjoy it—if indeed it is a thing and not the cause of all things, and if indeed it is a cause. It is not easy to find a suitable name for such excellence, but perhaps the Trinity is better called the one God from whom, through whom, and in whom

11 everything is [Rom. 11: 36]. There is the Father and the Son and the Holy Spirit—each one of these is God, and all of them together are one God; each of these is a full substance and all together are one substance. The Father is neither the Son nor the Holy Spirit, the Son is neither the Father nor the Holy Spirit, the Holy Spirit is neither the Father nor the Son, but the Father is purely the Father, the Son purely the Son, and

12 the Holy Spirit purely the Holy Spirit. These three have the same eternal nature, the same unchangeableness, the same majesty, the same power. In the Father there is unity, in the Son equality, and in the Holy Spirit a harmony of unity and equality. And the three are all one because of the Father, all equal because of the Son, and all in harmony because of the Holy Spirit.

13   Have I spoken something, have I uttered something, worthy of God? No, I feel that all I have done is to wish to speak; if I did say something, it is not what I wanted to say. How do I know this? Simply because God is unspeakable. But what I have spoken would not have been spoken if it were unspeakable. For this reason God should not even be called unspeakable, because even when this word is spoken, something is spoken. There is a kind of conflict between words here:* if what cannot be spoken is unspeakable, then it is not unspeakable, because it can actually be said to be unspeakable. It is better to evade this verbal conflict silently than to quell it disputatiously.

Yet although nothing can be spoken in a way worthy of God, he   14
has sanctioned the homage of the human voice, and chosen
that we should derive pleasure from our words in praise of him.
Hence the fact that he is called God: he himself is not truly
known by the sound of these two syllables,* yet when the
sound strikes the ear it leads all users of the Latin language to
think of a supremely excellent and immortal being.

Now although he alone is thought of as the god of gods, he is   15
also thought of by those who imagine, invoke, and worship
other gods, whether in heaven or on earth, in so far as their
thinking strives to reach a being than which there is nothing
better or more exalted. They are, to be sure, inspired by various ideas of excellence, of which some relate to the senses, and
others to the intellect, and accordingly those who are devoted
to the bodily senses* think that either the sky itself, or the
brightest element that they see in the sky, or the world itself, is
the god of gods. If they try to pass beyond the visible world,
they envisage something bright, and in their futile imagin-
ations represent it either as an infinite being or as one endowed
with what they see as ultimate beauty; or else they think of the
figure of a human body, if they value that above all else. If they   16
do not believe in a single god of gods, but rather in many gods,
or gods without number, all of them having equal status, then
for these too they form a mental picture which corresponds to
their various ideas of bodily excellence. Those who strive to
behold the nature of God through their intellect* place him
above all visible and corporeal beings, indeed above all intelligible and spiritual beings, and above all beings that are subject
to change. But they all vigorously contend for the excellence of
God; it is impossible to find anyone who believes that God is a
thing than which there exists something better. All, then, are
agreed that what they value above all other things is God.

And since all who think of God think of something alive, the   17
only thinkers whose conceptions of God are not absurd and
unworthy can be those who think of life itself. Whatever corporeal form occurs to them, they establish that it either lives or
does not live; and they esteem what lives more highly than
what does not. They understand that the living corporeal
form, however outstanding its light, however outstanding its

size, however outstanding its beauty, consists of two separate
things, namely itself and the life by which it is energized; and
they raise that life above the mass which is energized and acti-
18 vated by it to a position of unrivalled status. Then they proceed
to examine that life, and if they find it has energy but not sense
(as in the case of trees) they subordinate it to a sentient form of
life (like that of livestock), and they subordinate that in turn to
an intelligent form of life (like that of humans). Realizing the
mutability of human life, they are obliged to subordinate that
too to some unchangeable form of life, namely the life which is
19 not intermittently wise but rather is wisdom itself.* A wise
mind (in other words, one that has acquired wisdom) was not
wise before it acquired wisdom; but wisdom itself was never
unwise, and never can be.* If they did not see this, they could
not, with such complete confidence, subordinate the changeable form of life to a form of life that was unchangeably wise.
They certainly see that the actual standard of truth,* by which
they maintain the superiority of that life, is not subject to
change, and they can only see this as belonging to a realm above
their own nature, since they see themselves to be subject to
20 change. Nobody is so brazenly stupid as to say, 'how do you
know that the form of life that is unchangeably wise is to be
ranked more highly than the changeable form?' The answer to
his question, about how I know, is publicly and unchangeably
present for all to behold. Anyone who fails to see this is like a
blind man in the sun, who cannot be helped by the brightness
21 of such a clear and powerful light shining into his eyes. But
someone who sees this yet runs away from it has a mind whose
insight is weakened by his habit of living in the shadows cast by
the flesh. Those, then, who follow what is secondary and inferior to whatever they admit to be better and more outstanding
are, as it were, blown away from their homeland by the adverse
winds of their own perverted characters.
22   Since, therefore, we must enjoy to the full that truth which
lives unchangeably, and since, within it, God the Trinity, the
author and creator of everything, takes thought for the things
that he has created, our minds must be purified* so that they
are able to perceive that light and then hold fast to it. Let us
consider this process of cleansing as a trek, or a voyage, to our

homeland;* though progress towards the one who is ever
present is not made through space, but through integrity
of purpose and character. This we would be unable to do, if 23
wisdom itself had not deigned to adapt itself to our great
weakness and offered us a pattern for living; and it has actually
done so in human form because we too are human. But because
we act wisely when we come to wisdom, wisdom has been
thought by arrogant people to have somehow acted foolishly
when it came to us; and because we recover strength when we
come to wisdom, wisdom has been reckoned as being somehow
weak when it came to us. But 'the foolishness of God is wiser
than men, and the weakness of God is stronger than men'
[1 Cor. 1: 25]. So although it is actually our homeland, it has
also made itself the road to our homeland. And although 24
wisdom is everywhere present to the inner eye that is healthy
and pure, it deigned to appear even to the carnal eyes of those
whose inner eye was weak and impure. For because 'in the
wisdom of God the world was incapable of recognizing God
through wisdom, it pleased God to save those who believe
through the foolishness of preaching' [1 Cor. 1: 21]. It is not, 25
then, by coming in a spatial sense but by appearing to mortals
in mortal flesh that wisdom is said to have come to us. So it
came to where it already was, because 'it was in this world and
the world was made through it' [John 1: 10]. But since human
beings, assimilated as they were to this world [Rom. 12: 2]
because of their desire to enjoy the created order instead of its
actual creator—and so very aptly described by the word
'world'—did not recognize it, the evangelist said, 'and the
world did not recognize it' [John 1: 10]. So, 'in the wisdom of
God the world was incapable of recognizing God through
wisdom' [1 Cor. 1: 21]. What then, since he was here already,
was the reason for his coming, if not that it pleased God to save
those who believed through the foolishness of preaching? And 26
what was the manner of his coming, if not this: 'The word was
made flesh and lived among us' [John 1: 14]? When we speak,
the word which we hold in our mind becomes a sound in order
that what we have in our mind may pass through ears of flesh
into the listener's mind: this is called speech. Our thought,
however, is not converted into the same sound, but remains

intact in its own home, suffering no diminution from its change* as it takes on the form of a word in order to make its way into the ears. In the same way the word of God became flesh in order to live in us but was unchanged.

27   The way to health is through medical care; God's care has taken it upon itself to heal and restore sinners by the same methods. When doctors bind wounds, they do this not just anyhow, but in an appropriate manner, so that the effectiveness of the dressing is matched by a kind of beauty; similarly the treatment given by wisdom was adapted to our wounds by its acceptance of human nature, healing sometimes by the
28   principle of contrariety, sometimes by that of similarity. A doctor treating a physical wound applies some medications that are contrary—a cold one to a hot wound, a dry one to a wet wound, and so on—and also some that are similar, such as a round bandage to a round wound and a rectangular bandage to a rectangular wound, and he does not apply the same dressing to all wounds, but matches like with like. So for the treatment of human beings God's wisdom—in itself both doctor and medicine—offered itself in a similar way. Because human beings fell through pride it used humility in healing them. We were deceived by the wisdom of the serpent; we are freed by
29   the foolishness of God. But just as that was called wisdom yet was foolishness to those who despised God, so this so-called foolishness is wisdom to those who overcome the devil. We made bad use of immortality, and so we died; Christ made good use of mortality, and so we live. The disease entered through a corrupted female mind; healing emerged from an intact female body. Also relevant to the principle of contrariety is the fact that our vices too are treated by the example of his
30   virtues. Examples of similarity in the kinds of bandages (as it were) applied to our limbs and wounds are these: it was one born of a woman that freed those deceived by a woman; it was a mortal man that freed mortals; and it was by death that he freed the dead. Careful consideration of many other such things (which can be done by those who are not hard-pressed by the need to finish a book!) reveals that the basic principle of Christian healing is one of contrariety and similarity.

31   Now the belief in the Lord's resurrection from the dead and

his ascent into heaven reinforces our faith with a great hope. It shows clearly how willingly he laid down his life for us [cf. John 10: 18], since he had it in his power to take it up again. What great confidence do believers have to buttress their hopes, when they consider the mighty things that such a mighty one suffered for those who did not yet believe! And as he is expected to come from heaven as judge of the living and the dead, he instils great fear into the uncommitted, so that they may develop a serious commitment and yearn for him in lives of goodness rather than fear him in lives of wickedness. For 32 what words can express, and what thoughts can conceive, the reward which he is going to give at the end? He has already given us so much of his spirit to support us on our journey, in order that in the troubles of this life we may have this enormous confidence and delight in one whom we do not yet behold; he has also bestowed individual gifts for the consolation of his church [1 Cor. 12: 7], in order that we may perform the tasks that he has indicated not only without murmuring but even with positive enjoyment. The church is his body, as 33 the teaching of the apostle shows [Eph. 1: 23]; it is also called his bride [Eph. 5: 22]. So he ties together his own body, with its many members performing different tasks [cf. Rom. 12: 4], in a bond of unity and love like a healing bandage. And at the present time he trains it and purges it by means of various disagreeable medicines so that when it has been saved from the world he may take as his wife for eternity 'the church, which has no spot or wrinkle or any such thing' [Eph. 5: 27].

Furthermore, given that we are on a road—in spiritual, 34 not spatial terms—and one blocked as it were by thorny hedgerows, which flourish through the evil influences of our earlier sins, could he who chose to lay himself down as the way by which we could return have done anything more generous and merciful than to forgive the converted all their sins and, by being crucified for us, pull out the firmly fixed barriers to our return? He accordingly gave keys to his church so that what- 35 ever it loosed on earth should also be loosed in heaven, and whatever it bound on earth should also be bound in heaven [Matt. 16: 19]. So that if anyone does not believe that his sins are forgiven in God's church they are not forgiven, but if anyone does believe and reform, turning from them to the right way, he is healed, within the bosom of the same church, by the very act of believing and reform. A person who does not believe that his sins can be forgiven is made worse by despair, feeling that nothing better awaits him than to be wicked, since he has no faith in the results of being converted.

36   Now just as the abandonment of one's earlier life and behaviour, which comes by repentance, is a sort of death of the soul, so too the dissolution of one's former mode of existence is the death of the body. And just as the soul is reformed after repentance, by which the soul kills off its earlier evil character, so we must believe and hope that after this death, to which we are all liable by the bondage of sin, the body is changed to something better at the time of resurrection. This will not mean that flesh and blood take over the kingdom of heaven—this is impossible [1 Cor. 15: 50]—but that this corruptible thing will put on incorruptibility and this mortal thing immortality [1 Cor. 15: 53], and that without making any trouble (for it will experience no deprivation) it will be energized by its blessed and perfect soul in

37   supreme tranquillity. If a person's soul does not die to the present world and begin to be conformed to the truth, it is drawn by the death of the body into a worse death and reborn not to experience a new heavenly state but to suffer the retri-

38   bution of punishment. This is contained in our faith, and this, we must believe, is the reality: neither the soul nor the human body suffers total destruction, but the wicked rise to unimaginable agony, the good to eternal life.

39   Among all these things, then, it is only the eternal and unchangeable things which I mentioned that are to be enjoyed; other things are to be used so that we may attain the full enjoyment of those things. We ourselves who enjoy and use other things are things. A human being is a major kind of thing, being made 'in the image and likeness of God' [Gen. 1: 26–7] not by virtue of having a mortal body but by virtue of having a

40   rational soul and thus a higher status than animals. It is therefore an important question whether humans should enjoy one another or use one another, or both.* We have been commanded to love one another [John 13: 34; 15: 12, 17], but the question is whether one person should be loved by another on

his own account or for some other reason. If on his own account, we enjoy him; if for some other reason, we use him. In my opinion, he should be loved for another reason. For if something is to be loved on its own account, it is made to constitute the happy life, even if it is not as yet the reality but the hope of it which consoles us at this time. But 'cursed is he who puts his hope in a man' [Jer. 17: 5].

Neither should a person enjoy himself, if you think closely 41 about this, because he should not love himself on his own account, but only on account of the one who is to be enjoyed. A person is at his best when in his whole life he strives towards the unchangeable form of life and holds fast to it wholeheartedly. But if he loves himself on his own account, he does not relate himself to God, but turns to himself and not to something unchangeable. And for this reason it is with a certain insufficiency that he enjoys himself, because when totally absorbed and controlled by the unchangeable good he is a better man than when his attention leaves it, even if it turns to himself. So if you ought to love yourself not on your 42 own account but on account of the one who is the most proper object of your love, another person should not be angry if you love him too on account of God. For the divinely established rule of love says 'you shall love your neighbour as yourself' but God 'with all your heart, and with all your soul, and with all your mind' [Matt. 22: 39, 37], so that you may devote all your thoughts and all your life and all your understanding to the one from whom you actually receive what you devote to him. And when it says 'all your heart, all your soul, 43 all your mind', it leaves no part of our life free from this obligation, no part free as it were to back out and enjoy some other thing; any other object of love that enters the mind should be swept towards the same destination as that to which the whole flood of our love is directed. So a person who loves his neighbour properly should, in concert with him, aim to love God with all his heart, all his soul, and all his mind. In this way, loving him as he would himself, he relates his love of himself and his neighbour entirely to the love of God, which allows not the slightest trickle to flow away from it and thereby diminish it.

44   It is not the case that all things which are to be used are to be loved; but only those which exist in some kind of association with us and are related to God, like a man or an angel, or which, being related to us, stand in need of the kindness of God as received through us, like the body. The martyrs, certainly, did not love the wickedness of those who persecuted them, but

45   used it to win their way to God. There are four things that are to be loved—one, that which is above us; two, that which we are; three, that which is close to us; four, that which is beneath us. No commandments needed to be given about the second and fourth of these. For however much a man may lapse from the truth, he retains a love of himself and a love of his own body. The mind which shuns the unchangeable light which is sovereign over all aims to exercise sovereignty over itself and its body, and so cannot fail to love both itself and its body.

46   And it thinks it has achieved something great if it can also dominate its peers, by which I mean other men. For it is the instinct of a corrupt mind to covet and claim as its due what is really due to God alone. This kind of self-love is better called hatred. It is unjust because it wants what is beneath it to serve it while itself refusing to serve what is above it; and it has been very well said that 'the person who loves injustice hates his own soul' [Ps. 10: 6 (11: 5)]. For this reason such a mind becomes

47   weak and is tormented because of its mortal body, for it is inevitable that it should love the body and be weighed down by the body's corruption. A body's immortality and immunity from corruption derives from health of mind, and health of mind means resolutely holding fast to something better, namely the unchangeable God. But when it aspires to dominate those who are its natural peers, that is, its fellow men, its arrogance is quite intolerable.

48   So nobody hates himself. On this point there has never been any dispute with any sect. But neither does anyone hate his own body. What the apostle said is true: 'no one ever felt hatred for his own body' [Eph. 5: 29]. Some say that they would prefer not to have a body at all, but they are mistaken. For what they hate is not their body, but its imperfections and its dead

49   weight. What they want is not to have no body at all, but to have one free from corruption and totally responsive; they

think that if the body were such a thing it would not be a body, because they consider such a thing to be a soul. When they seem to persecute their own body by a kind of repression, and by hardships, their aim (if they are doing it rightly) is not to have no body at all but to have one that is subservient and ready for necessary tasks. It is the lusts which misuse the body—in 50 other words, the habits and inclinations of a soul to enjoy what is inferior*—that they are trying to eliminate by this strenuous drilling of the body itself. After all, they do not kill themselves, and have some concern for their health.

Those who have this misguided aim are waging war on their 51 body as if it were a natural enemy. They are misled by their reading of the words 'the flesh lusts against the spirit and the spirit against the flesh; for these are in conflict with each other' [Gal. 5: 17]. These words were spoken because of the ungovernable habits of the flesh, against which the spirit lusts not in order to destroy the body but to make it subservient to the spirit, as our nature demands, by taming its lusts, that is, its evil habits. For since it will be the case after the resurrection 52 that the body will live for ever in a state of utmost tranquillity and total subservience to the spirit, it should be our concern in this life that the tendency of the flesh is reformed and not allowed to resist the spirit with its unruly impulses. But until this happens, the flesh lusts against the spirit and the spirit against the flesh. The spirit fights back not out of hatred, but to establish its primacy, because it wants the body it loves to be subservient to something better; nor does the flesh fight back out of hatred, but because of the stranglehold of these habits which, after establishing themselves in the stock of our ancestors, have become naturally ingrained. The spirit's aim in sub- 53 duing the flesh is to break the perverse contracts* (so to speak) of these evil habits and establish the peace brought by good habits. Even those who are corrupted by false ideas and hate their bodies would not be prepared to lose one eye (no, not even painlessly, and not even if the sight remaining in the other eye were as good as the sight that there had been in both), unless constrained by some greater necessity. This and other arguments make it clear enough to those who seek the truth without prejudice that the apostle's judgement was sound when he said 'no one ever felt hatred for his own body' [Eph. 5: 29]. And he added, 'but one feeds it and looks after it, as Christ did to the church'.

54   Human beings must also be told how to love, that is, how to love themselves so as to do themselves good. (It would be absurd to doubt that anyone wishes to love himself and do himself good.) They must also be told how to love their own bodies so as to look after them systematically and sensibly; for it is equally obvious that one loves one's own body and wants it to

55 be healthy and sound. Now it is possible to love something more than the health and soundness of one's own body. It is well known that many people have voluntarily undergone pain and the amputation of limbs in order to obtain other things which they valued more. But it should not be said that someone does not value his body's health and safety just because he

56 values something else more highly. A miser buys himself bread in spite of the fact that he loves money; in doing so he gives away the money which he loves so much and wants to have more of, but he does this because he puts a greater value on the health of his body, which needs the bread for its sustenance. It is pointless to discuss such an obvious point further—though the heresy of the wicked often leaves us with no choice.

57   There is, then, no need to be instructed to love oneself and one's body; we love what we are and what is inferior to us but belongs to us, according to an immovable unvarying natural law, one which was also made for animals, because even animals love themselves and their bodies. It therefore remains for us to receive instruction about what is above us and what is close to us. Scripture says, 'You shall love the Lord your God with all your heart and with all your soul and with all your mind', and, 'you shall love your neighbour as yourself. On these two commandments depend the entire law and the

58 prophets' [Matt. 22: 37–40]. The aim of the commandment is love [cf. 1 Tim. 1: 5], a twofold love of God and of one's neighbour. But if you understand by this your whole person—mind and body—and your whole neighbour—that is, his mind and body, for a person consists of mind and body—no class of things to be loved is missing from these two commandments. Although love of God comes first and the manner of loving him

is clearly laid down, in such a way that everything else flows into it, nothing seems to have been said about self-love. But when it is said 'you shall love your neighbour as yourself', your own self-love is not neglected.

The person who lives a just and holy life is one who is a 59 sound judge of these things. He is also a person who has ordered his love,* so that he does not love what it is wrong to love, or fail to love what should be loved, or love too much what should be loved less (or love too little what should be loved more*), or love two things equally if one of them should be loved either less or more than the other, or love things either more or less if they should be loved equally. No sinner, *qua* sinner, should be loved; every human being, *qua* human being, should be loved on God's account; and God should be loved for himself. And if God is to be loved more than any human 60 being, each person should love God more than he loves himself. Likewise, another human being should be loved more than our own bodies, because all these things are to be loved on account of God whereas another person can enjoy God together with us in a way in which the body cannot, since the body lives only through the soul, and it is the soul by which we enjoy God.

All people should be loved equally. But you cannot do good 61 to all people equally, so you should take particular thought for those who, as if by lot, happen to be particularly close to you in terms of place, time, or any other circumstances. Suppose that 62 you had plenty of something which had to be given to someone in need of it but could not be given to two people, and you met two people, neither of whom had a greater need or a closer relationship to you than the other: you could do nothing more just than to choose by lot the person to whom you should give what could not be given to both. Analogously, since you cannot take thought for all men, you must settle (rather than by lot) in favour of the one who happens to be more closely associated with you in temporal matters.

Of all those who are capable of enjoying God together with 63 us, we love some whom we are helping, and some who are helping us; some whose help we need and some whose needs we are meeting; some to whom we give no benefit and some by whom

we do not expect any benefit to be given to us. But it should be our desire that they all love God together with us, and all the help that we give to or receive from them must be related to this
64 one end. In the theatre—that den of wickedness*—someone who loves an actor and revels in his skill as if it were a great good, or even the supreme one, also loves all those who share his love, not on their account, but on account of the one they equally love. The more passionate he is in his love, the more he tries by whatever methods he can to make his hero loved by a greater number of people, and the more he desires to point him out to a greater number of people. If he sees someone unenthusiastic he rouses him with his praises as much as he can. If he finds anyone antagonistic, he violently hates that person's hatred of his hero and goes all out to remove it by whatever methods he can. So what should we do in sharing the love of God, whose full enjoyment constitutes the happy life? It is God from whom all those who love him derive both their existence and their love; it is God who frees us from any fear that he can fail to satisfy anyone to whom he becomes known; it is God who wants himself to be loved, not in order to gain any reward for himself but to give to those who love him an eternal
65 reward—namely himself, the object of their love. Hence the fact that we also love our enemies. We do not fear them, for they cannot take away from us what we love, but we pity them, for they hate us all the more because they are separated from the one we love. If they turned to him, it is inevitable that they would love him as the goodness which is the source of all happiness and love us as joint participants in such goodness.

66   At this point there arise questions about the angels. They are happy because they enjoy the one whom we too desire to enjoy; and the more we enjoy him in this life, whether 'in a mirror' or 'obscurely' [1 Cor. 13: 12], the easier it is for us to endure our absence and the stronger our yearning to end it. But it may be asked, not unreasonably, whether love of the
67 angels is also covered by these two commandments. That the commandment to love our neighbour excludes no human being is made clear by our Lord himself in the gospel and by the apostle Paul. When our Lord was asked 'And who is my neighbour?' [Luke 10: 29] by the man to whom he had

pronounced these same two commandments and said that the whole law and the prophets depended on them [Matt. 22: 37–40], he told the story of a man going down from Jerusalem to Jericho who fell among thieves, was badly beaten up by them, and left injured and half-dead. He taught that the man's only neighbour was the man who showed kindness in reviving and healing him; and he put this in such a way that when questioned the questioner himself admitted it. The Lord 68 said to him, 'Go and do the same' [Luke 10: 37]; so it is clear that we should understand by our neighbour the person to whom an act of compassion is due if he needs it or would be due if he needed it. It follows from this that a person from whom an act of compassion is due to us in our turn is also our neighbour. For the word 'neighbour' implies a relationship: one can only be a neighbour to a neighbour. Who can fail to see that there is 69 no exception to this, nobody to whom compassion is not due? The commandment extends even to our enemies; in the words of our Lord once again, 'Love your enemies, do good to those who hate you' [Matt. 5: 44]. This is also the teaching of the 70 apostle Paul when he says, 'The commandments "You shall not commit adultery, you shall not kill, you shall not steal, you shall not covet," and any other commandment, are summed up in this text: "You shall love your neighbour as yourself." The love of one's neighbour does no wrong' [Rom. 13: 9–10]. Anyone who thinks that the apostle was not here giving commandments that embraced all people is compelled to admit something totally absurd and totally wicked: that Paul thought it no sin to violate the wife of a non-Christian or an enemy, or to kill him or covet his property. If this conclusion is absurd, it is clear that all people must be reckoned as neighbours, because evil must not be done to anyone.

So if the person to whom compassion must be shown and 71 the person by whom it must be shown to us are rightly called neighbours, it is obvious that the commandment by which we are instructed to love our neighbour also embraces the holy angels, who perform so many acts of compassion on our behalf, as can easily be observed in many passages of the holy scriptures. It follows that even the Lord God himself wanted to be called our neighbour; for the Lord Jesus Christ made clear that

it was he himself who assisted the man who lay half-dead on the
72 road, beaten up and abandoned by the robbers. And in a prayer
the prophet says, 'I grieved for him as for a neighbour, or a
brother' [Ps. 34: 14 (35: 14)]. But because the divine substance
is altogether transcendent and far above our own nature, the
commandment to love God was kept distinct from the commandment to love our neighbour. God shows compassion to us
because of his own kindness, and we in turn show it to one
another because of his kindness: in other words, he pities us so
that we may enjoy him, and we in our turn pity one another so
that we may enjoy him.

73   There is still an element of uncertainty here. I am saying that
we enjoy a thing which we love for itself, and that we should
enjoy only a thing by which we are made happy, but use everything else. God loves us (and the divine scripture often com-
mends his love towards us) [cf. Rom. 5: 8], but in what way
74 does he love us—so as to use us or to enjoy us? If he enjoys us,
he stands in need of our goodness, which only a madman could
assert; for all our goodness either comes from him or actually
consists of him. Is it not quite clear and beyond all doubt that
light does not stand in need of the brightness of the things
which it illuminates? The prophet says very clearly, 'I said to
the Lord, "You are my Lord, since you do not stand in need of
my goodness" ' [Ps. 15: 2 (16: 2)]. So God does not enjoy us,
but uses us. (If he neither enjoys nor uses us, then I fail to see
how he can love us at all.)

75   But he does not use us in the way that we use things; for we
relate the things which we use to the aim of enjoying God's
goodness, whereas God relates his use of us to his own goodness. We exist because he is good, and we are good to the extent
that we exist. Moreover, because he is also just, we are not evil
with impunity; if we are evil, to that extent we exist less. God
exists in the supreme sense, and the original sense, of the word.
He is altogether unchangeable, and it is he who could say with
full authority 'I am who I am', and 'You will say to them, "I
have been sent by the one who is" ' [Exod. 3: 14]; so it is true of
other things which exist that they could not exist except by
him, and that they are good to the extent that they have
76 received their existence from him. So the kind of use attributed

to God, that by which he uses us, is related not to his own advantage, but solely to his goodness. If we pity someone or take thought for someone, we do so for that person's advantage, and we concentrate on that; but somehow there also results an advantage to us, since God does not let the compassion we show to the needy go unrewarded. This reward is the supreme reward—that we may thoroughly enjoy him and that all of us who enjoy him may enjoy one another in him.

For if we enjoy one another in ourselves, we remain as it 77 were on the road and put our hopes of happiness on a human being or an angel. This is something that arrogant people and arrogant angels pride themselves on; they rejoice when the hopes of others are placed on them. But a holy person or a holy angel restores us when we are weary and when we desire to rest in them and stay with them, using either the resources which they have received for our sakes or those which they have received for their own sakes (but in either case they have certainly received them); and then they impel us, thus restored, to go to the one by enjoying whom we likewise are made happy. The apostle exclaims, 'Was it Paul that was crucified for 78 you? Or were you baptized in Paul's name?' [1 Cor. 1: 13] and 'Neither he who plants nor he who waters is anything, but only God who gives the increase' [1 Cor. 3: 7]. And the angel warned the man who was adoring him to adore God instead, as the master under whom he was but the man's fellow servant [Rev. 19: 10; 22: 8–9].

When you enjoy a human being in God, you are enjoying 79 God rather than that human being. For you enjoy the one by whom you are made happy, and you will one day rejoice that you have attained the one in whom you now set your hope of attaining him. So Paul says to Philemon: 'So, brother, I shall enjoy you in the Lord'* [Philem. 20]. If he had not added the words 'in the Lord', and just said 'I shall enjoy you', he would have been setting his hopes of happiness on Philemon. Yet the idea of enjoying someone or something is very close to that of using someone or something together with love. For when the 80 object of love is present, it inevitably brings with it pleasure as well. If you go beyond this pleasure and relate it to your permanent goal, you are using it, and are said to enjoy it not in

the literal sense but in a transferred sense.* But if you hold fast
and go no further, making it the goal of your joy, then you
should be described as enjoying it in the true and literal sense
of the word. This is to be done only in the case of the Trinity,
the supreme and unchangeable good.

81   Although the truth itself and the word by which all things
were made became flesh so that it could live among us [John
1: 3, 14], notice how the apostle says, 'And if we knew Christ
according to the flesh, we do not know him in the same way
now' [2 Cor. 5: 16]. In fact Christ, who chose to offer himself
not only as a possession for those who come to their journey's
end but also as a road for those who come to the beginning of
the ways, chose to become flesh. Whence the saying, 'God created me at the beginning of his ways' [Prov. 8: 22], so that those
82   who wanted to come could begin from there. The apostle,
then, although still walking on the road and following God as
he called him to the prize of a higher calling, none the less 'forgetting what was behind and straining forward to what lay
ahead' [Phil. 3: 14, 13] had already passed beyond the beginning of the ways. In other words, he was not deprived of the
one from whom the journey must actually be undertaken and
begun by all who long to come to the truth and abide in eternal
life. For Christ says, 'I am the way, the truth, and the life' [John
14: 6]; that is, 'you come by me, you come to me, you abide in
83   me.' For when you come to him, you come also to the Father
[cf. John 14: 6–11], because God, to whom he is equal, is recognized through his equal, and the spirit binds us and as it were
cements us together, so that we can abide in the supreme and
unchangeable good. From this it is to be inferred that nothing
must detain us on our way, since not even the Lord, at least in
his graciously chosen role of being our way, wanted to detain
us; rather he wanted us to pass on, not sticking feebly to temporal things—even though they were accepted and endured by
him for our salvation—but hastening eagerly through them so
that we may achieve progress and success in our journey to the
one who has freed our nature from temporal things and set it at
the Father's right hand.

84   The chief purpose of all that we have been saying in our discussion of things is to make it understood that the fulfilment

and end of the law [cf. Rom. 13: 10; 1 Tim. 1: 5] and all the
divine scriptures is to love the thing which must be enjoyed
and the thing which together with us can enjoy that thing
(since there is no need for a commandment to love oneself). To 85
enlighten us and enable us, the whole temporal dispensation
was set up by divine providence for our salvation. We must
make use of this, not with a permanent love and enjoyment of
it, but with a transient love and enjoyment of our journey, or of
our conveyances, so to speak, or any other expedients whatso-
ever (there may be a more appropriate word), so that we love
the means of transport only because of our destination.

So anyone who thinks that he has understood the divine 86
scriptures or any part of them, but cannot by his understanding build up this double love of God and neighbour, has not yet
succeeded in understanding them. Anyone who derives from
them an idea which is useful for supporting this love but fails to
say what the writer demonstrably meant in the passage has not
made a fatal error, and is certainly not a liar. In a liar there is a
desire to say what is false, and that is why we find many who
want to lie but nobody who wants to be misled.* Since a person 87
lies knowingly but is misled unknowingly, it is clear enough
that in any given situation the person misled is better than the
one who lies, since it is better to suffer injustice than to commit
it. Everyone who lies commits injustice; so anyone who
believes that a lie is sometimes useful believes that injustice is
sometimes useful. No one who lies keeps faith while lying—he
certainly desires that the person he lies to should put faith in
him, but when lying he does not keep faith—and everyone who
breaks faith is unjust. So either injustice is sometimes useful—
which is impossible—or lying is always useless. Anyone with 88
an interpretation of the scriptures that differs from that of the
writer is misled, but not because the scriptures are lying. If, as
I began by saying, he is misled by an idea of the kind that builds
up love, which is the end of the commandment, he is misled in
the same way as a walker who leaves his path by mistake but
reaches the destination to which the path leads by going
through a field. But he must be put right and shown how it is
more useful not to leave the path, in case the habit of deviating
should force him to go astray or even adrift.

89   It often happens that by thoughtlessly asserting something
that the author did not mean an interpreter runs up against
other things which cannot be reconciled with that original
idea. If he agrees that these things are true and certain, his original interpretation could not possibly be true, and by cherish-
ing his own idea he comes in some strange way to be more
displeased with scripture than with himself. If he encourages
this evil to spread it will be his downfall. For 'we walk by faith,
not by sight' [2 Cor. 5: 7], and faith will falter if the authority of
holy scripture is shaken; and if faith falters, love itself decays.

90   For if someone lapses in his faith, he inevitably lapses in his
love as well, since he cannot love what he does not believe to be
true. If on the other hand he both believes and loves, then by
good conduct and by following the rules of good behaviour he
gives himself reason to hope that he will attain what he loves.
So there are these three things which all knowledge and

91   prophecy serve: faith, hope, and love [1 Cor. 13: 13]. But faith
will be replaced by the sight of visible reality, and hope by the
real happiness which we shall attain, whereas love will actually
increase when these things pass away. If, through faith, we love
what we cannot yet see, how much greater will our love be
when we have begun to see! And if, through hope, we love
something that we have not yet attained, how much greater

92   will our love be when we have attained it! There is this important difference between temporal things and eternal things:
something temporal is loved more before it is possessed, but
will lose its appeal when attained, for it does not satisfy the
soul, whose true and certain abode is eternity. The eternal, on
the other hand, is loved more passionately when obtained than
when desired. No one who desires it is allowed to think more
highly of it than is warranted (it would then disappoint when
found to be less impressive); but however high one's expectations while on the way, one will find it even more impressive
on arrival.

93   Therefore a person strengthened by faith, hope, and love,
and who steadfastly holds on to them, has no need of the scriptures except to instruct others. That is why many people, rely-
ing on these three things, actually live in solitude without any
texts of the scriptures. They are, I think, a fulfilment of the

saying 'If there are prophecies, they will lose their meaning; if there are tongues, they will cease; if there is knowledge that too will lose its meaning' [1 Cor. 13: 8]. By this machinery (so to 94 speak) such an edifice of faith, hope, and love has been built in them that they do not seek what is imperfect [1 Cor. 13: 10], for they hold what is perfect—perfect, that is, as far as anything can be in this life; for in comparison with the life to come the life of no righteous or holy man in this world is perfect. This is why scripture says, 'there remain faith, hope, and love, these three; the greatest of these is love' [1 Cor. 13: 13]: when one reaches eternity the other two will pass away and love will remain in an enhanced and a more certain form.

So when someone has learnt that the aim of the command- 95 ment is 'love from a pure heart, and good conscience and genuine faith' [1 Tim. 1: 5], he will be ready to relate every interpretation of the holy scriptures to these three things and may approach the task of handling these books with confidence. For when the apostle said 'love' he added 'from a pure heart', so that nothing is loved except what should be loved. He added 'good' to 'conscience' because of hope; for a person with the incubus of a bad conscience despairs of reaching what he loves and believes. Thirdly, he said 'with genuine faith': for if 96 our faith is free of untruthfulness then we do not love what should not be loved, whereas by living aright it is impossible for our hope to be in any way misguided. I have chosen to speak of the things which are objects of our faith only to the extent that I considered necessary for the present context; much has already been said by me and by others in other works. This is the end of this book. The remainder of my discussion, in as much detail as the Lord allows, will be about signs.

BOOK TWO

1 When I was writing about things I began with the warning that attention should be paid solely to the fact that they existed, and not to anything besides themselves that they might signify.* Now that I am discussing signs, I must say, conversely, that attention should not be paid to the fact that they exist, but rather to the fact that they are signs, or, in other words, that they signify.* For a sign is a thing which of itself makes some other thing come to mind, besides the impression that it presents to the senses. So when we see a footprint we think that the animal whose footprint it is has passed by; when we see smoke we realize that there is fire beneath it; when we hear the voice of an animate being we observe its feeling; and when the trumpet sounds soldiers know they must advance or retreat or do whatever else the state of the battle demands.

2   Some signs are natural, others given. Natural signs are those which without a wish or any urge to signify cause something else besides themselves to be known from them, like smoke, which signifies fire. It does not signify fire because it wishes to do so; but because of our observation and consideration of things previously experienced it is realized that there is fire beneath it, even if nothing but smoke appears. The footprint of a passing animal also belongs to this category. The expression of an angry or depressed person signifies an emotional state even if there is no such wish on the part of the person who is angry or depressed, and likewise any other emotion is revealed by the evidence of the face even if we are not seeking to reveal it. It is not my intention to discuss this whole category now, but since it comes into my classification it could not be omitted altogether. So let the above remarks suffice.

3   Given signs are those which living things give to each other, in order to show, to the best of their ability, the emotions of their minds, or anything that they have felt or learnt. There is no reason for us to signify something (that is, to give a sign) except to express and transmit to another's mind what is in the mind of the person who gives the sign. It is this category of

signs—to the extent that it applies to humans—that I have decided to examine and discuss, because even the divinely given signs contained in the holy scriptures have been communicated to us by the human beings who wrote them. Some 4 animals, too, have signs among themselves by which they show the desires of their minds: a cockerel on finding food gives a vocal sign to its hen to come quickly, and a dove calls to, or is called by, its mate by cooing. Many other such signs are observed regularly. Whether (as with a facial expression or a shout of pain) they accompany emotion without any desire to signify, or whether they are really given in order to signify something, is another question, and irrelevant to the matter in hand. I am excluding it from this work as not essential.

Some of the signs by which people communicate their 5 feelings to one another concern the eyes; most of them concern the ears, and a very small number concern the other senses. When we nod, we give a sign just to the eyes of the person whom we want, by means of that sign, to make aware of our wishes. Particular movements of the hands signify a great deal. By the movement of all their limbs, actors give certain signs to the cognoscenti and converse with the spectators' eyes, as it were; and it is through the eyes that flags and standards convey the wishes of military commanders. All these things are, to coin a phrase, visible words. But most signs, as I said, and espe- 6 cially verbal ones, concern the ears. A trumpet, a flute, and a lyre generally produce not just a pleasant sound but one that is also significant. But these signs are very few compared with words. Words have gained an altogether dominant role among humans in signifying the ideas conceived by the mind that a person wants to reveal. It is true that our Lord gave a sign 7 through the smell of the ointment by which his feet were anointed [John 12: 3–7], and that in the sacrament of his body and blood he signified his wishes through the sense of taste [Matt. 26: 26–8; Mark 14: 22–4; Luke 22: 15–20], and that the healing of the woman who touched the border of his garment [Matt. 9: 20–2; Mark 5: 25–9; Luke 8: 43–4] has its significance. But an incalculable number of the signs by which people disclose their thoughts consist in words. I have been able to express in words all the various kinds of sign that I have briefly mentioned, but in no way could I have expressed all my words in terms of signs.

8   But spoken words cease to exist as soon as they come into contact with the air, and their existence is no more lasting than that of their sound; hence the invention, in the form of letters, of signs of words. In this way words are presented to the eyes, not in themselves, but by certain signs peculiar to them. These signs could not be shared by all nations, because of the sin of human disunity by which each one sought hegemony for itself. This pride is signified by the famous tower raised towards heaven at the time when wicked men justly received incompatible languages to match their incompatible minds [Gen. 11: 1–9].

9   Consequently even divine scripture, by which assistance is provided for the many serious disorders of the human will, after starting off in a single language,* in which it could have been conveniently spread throughout the world, was circulated far and wide in the various languages of translators and became known in this way to the Gentiles for their salvation. The aim of its readers is simply to find out the thoughts and wishes of those by whom it was written down and, through them, the will of God, which we believe these men followed as they spoke.

10   But casual readers are misled by problems and ambiguities of many kinds, mistaking one thing for another. In some passages they find no meaning at all that they can grasp at, even falsely, so thick is the fog created by some obscure phrases. I have no doubt that this is all divinely predetermined, so that pride may be subdued by hard work and intellects which tend to despise things that are easily discovered may be rescued

11   from boredom and reinvigorated.* Suppose someone were to make the following statements: that there exist holy and perfect men by whose lives and conduct the church of Christ tears away those who come to it from their various superstitions, and somehow, by inspiring them to imitate their goodness, incorporates them into itself; and that there exist servants of the true God, good and faithful men who, putting aside the burdens of this life, have come to the holy font of baptism, arise from it born again with the Holy Spirit, and then produce the fruit of a double love, that is love of God and love of their neighbour.*

Why is it, I wonder, that putting it like this gives less pleasure to an audience than by expounding in the same terms this passage from the Song of Songs [S. of S. 4: 2], where the church is addressed and praised like a beautiful woman: 'Your teeth are like a flock of shorn ewes ascending from the pool, all of which give birth to twins, and there is not a sterile animal among them'? Surely one learns the same lesson as when one hears it 12 in plain words without the support of the imagery? And yet somehow it gives me more pleasure to contemplate holy men when I see them as the teeth of the church tearing men away from their errors and transferring them into its body, breaking down their rawness by biting and chewing. And it is with the greatest of pleasure that I visualize the shorn ewes, their worldly burdens set aside like fleeces, ascending from the pool (baptism) and all giving birth to twins (the two commandments of love), with none of them failing to produce this holy fruit. Exactly why this picture gives me greater pleasure than if 13 no such imagery were presented by the divine books, since the topic is the same, and the lesson the same, it is difficult to say; this, however, is another question entirely. But no one disputes that it is much more pleasant to learn lessons presented through imagery, and much more rewarding to discover meanings that are won only with difficulty. Those who fail to 14 discover what they are looking for suffer from hunger, whereas those who do not look, because they have it in front of them, often die of boredom. In both situations the danger is lethargy. It is a wonderful and beneficial thing that the Holy Spirit 15 organized the holy scripture so as to satisfy hunger by means of its plainer passages and remove boredom by means of its obscurer ones. Virtually nothing is unearthed from these obscurities which cannot be found quite plainly expressed somewhere else.

It is therefore necessary above all else to be moved by the 16 fear of God* towards learning his will: what it is that he instructs us to seek or avoid. This fear will necessarily inspire reflection about our mortality and future death, and by nailing our flesh to the wood of the cross as it were crucify all our presumptuous impulses. After that it is necessary, 17 through holiness, to become docile, and not contradict holy

scripture—whether we understand it (as when it hits at some
of our vices) or fail to understand it (as when we feel that we
could by ourselves gain better knowledge or give better
instruction)—but rather ponder and believe that what is written there, even if obscure, is better and truer than any insights
that we can gain by our own efforts.

18   After these two stages of fear and holiness comes the third
stage, that of knowledge, with which I now propose to deal.
This is the area in which every student of the divine scriptures
exerts himself, and what he will find in them is quite simply
that he must love God for himself, and his neighbour for God's
sake, and that he must love God with his whole heart, his whole
soul, and his whole mind, and his neighbour as himself [Matt.
22: 37–9]—in other words, that his love of his neighbour, like
19 his own self-love, should be totally related to God. (I have dealt
with these two commandments in the previous book, in my
discussion of things.) It is vital that the reader first learns from
the scriptures that he is entangled in a love of this present age,
of temporal things, that is, and is far from loving God and his
neighbour to the extent that scripture prescribes. It is at this
point that the fear which makes him ponder the judgement of
God, and the holiness which makes it impossible for him not to
admit and submit to the authority of the holy books, compel
20 him to deplore his own condition. For this knowledge makes a
person with good reason to hope not boastful but remorseful;
in this state he obtains by constant prayer the encouragement
of divine assistance, so that he is not crushed by despair. And
so he begins to be at the fourth stage—that of fortitude—
which brings a hunger and thirst after righteousness [Matt.
5: 6]. In this state he extricates himself from all the fatal charms
of transient things; turning away from these, he turns to the
love of eternal things, namely the unchangeable unity which is
also the Trinity.

21   When he beholds this light (as far as he is able to), shining as
it does even into remote places, and realizes that because of the
weakness of his vision he cannot bear its brilliance, he is at the
fifth stage—that is, in the resolve of compassion*—and purifies his mind, which is somehow turbulent and in conflict with
itself because of the impurities accumulated by its desire of

what is inferior. Here he strenuously occupies himself with the love of his neighbour and becomes perfect in it. Full of hope 22 now, and at full strength, since he has come to love even his enemy, he rises to the sixth stage, in which he now purifies the eye by which God may actually be seen—to the extent that he may be seen by those who, to the best of their ability, die to this world; for they see to the extent that they die to the world, and to the extent that they live in it they fail to see. The vision of that light, although it now begins to appear more steady and not only more tolerable but also more pleasant, is none the less said to be seen still obscurely and through a mirror [1 Cor. 13: 12]; this is because we walk more by faith than by sight [2 Cor. 5: 6–7] as we travel in this life, even though we are citizens of heaven [cf. Phil. 3: 20]. At this stage he purifies the eye of his 23 heart so that not even his neighbour is given a higher priority than the truth, or even an equal one; nor does he give priority to himself, since he does not give it to the one whom he loves as himself. So this holy person will have a heart so single-minded and purified that he will not be deflected from the truth either by an eagerness to please men or by the thought of avoiding any of the troubles which beset him in this life. Such a son ascends to wisdom, which is the seventh and last stage, enjoyed by those who are calm and peaceful. 'The fear of the Lord is the beginning of wisdom' [Ps. 110: 10 (111: 10)]: these are the stages by which we progress from the one to the other.

But let us take our thoughts back to the third stage. Here 24 I propose to discuss and consider whatever ideas the Lord may provide. The most expert investigator of the divine scriptures will be the person who, first, has read them all and has a good knowledge—a reading knowledge, at least, if not yet a complete understanding—of those pronounced canonical. He will read the others more confidently when equipped with a belief in the truth; they will then be unable to take possession of his unprotected mind and prejudice him in any way against sound interpretations or delude him by their dangerous falsehoods and fantasies. In the matter of canonical scriptures he should follow the authority of the great majority of catholic churches, including of course those that were found worthy to have apostolic seats and receive apostolic letters. He will apply this 25

principle to the canonical scriptures: to prefer those accepted
by all catholic churches to those which some do not accept. As
for those not universally accepted, he should prefer those
accepted by a majority of churches, and by the more authoritative ones, to those supported by fewer churches, or by
churches of lesser authority. Should he find that some scriptures are accepted by the majority of churches, but others by
the more authoritative ones (though in fact he could not possibly find this situation) I think that they should be considered
to have equal authority.

26   The complete canon of scripture,* on which I say that our
attention should be concentrated, includes the following
books: the five books of Moses (Genesis, Exodus, Leviticus,
Numbers, Deuteronomy), and the single books of Joshua, son
of Nave, and of Judges, and the little book known as Ruth,
which seems to relate more to the beginning of Kings, and then
the four books of Kings and the two of Chronicles, which do
not follow chronologically but proceed as it were side by side
27 with Kings. All this is historiography, which covers continuous periods of time and gives a chronological sequence of
events. There are others, forming another sequence, not connected with either this class or each other, like Job, Tobias,
Esther, Judith, and the two books of Maccabees and the two of
Ezra,* which rather seem to follow on from the chronologically
ordered account which ends with Kings and Chronicles. Then
come the prophets, including David's single book of Psalms,
and three books of Solomon, namely Proverbs, Song of Songs,
and Ecclesiastes. The two books entitled Wisdom and Ecclesi-
asticus are also said to be by Solomon, on the strength of a general similarity; but there is a strong tradition that Jesus Sirach
wrote them,* and, in any case, because they have been found
worthy of inclusion among authoritative texts, they should be
28 numbered with the prophetic books. There remain the books
of the prophets properly so called, the individual books of the
twelve prophets who because they are joined together and
never separated are counted as one. Their names are these:
Hosea, Joel, Amos, Obadiah, Jonah, Micah, Nahum,
Habakkuk, Zephaniah, Haggai, Zechariah, and Malachi. Then
there are the four prophets in larger books: Isaiah, Jeremiah,

Daniel, Ezekiel. These forty-four books form the authoritative   29
Old Testament; the authoritative New Testament consists of
the gospel in four books (Matthew, Mark, Luke, John), fourteen letters of the apostle Paul (Romans, Corinthians (two),
Galatians, Ephesians, Philippians, Thessalonians (two),
Colossians,* Timothy (two), Titus, Philemon, Hebrews), two
of Peter, three of John, one of Jude, and one of James; the single book of the Acts of the Apostles and the single book of the
Revelation of John.

These are all the books in which those who fear God and are   30
made docile by their holiness seek God's will. The first rule in
this laborious task is, as I have said, to know these books; not
necessarily to understand them but to read them so as to commit them to memory or at least make them not totally unfamiliar. Then the matters which are clearly stated in them, whether
ethical precepts or articles of belief, should be examined carefully and intelligently. The greater a person's intellectual
capacity, the more of these he finds. In clearly expressed   31
passages of scripture one can find all the things that concern
faith and the moral life (namely hope and love, treated in my
previous book*). Then, after gaining a familiarity with the language of the divine scriptures, one should proceed to explore
and analyse the obscure passages, by taking examples from the
more obvious parts to illuminate obscure expressions and by
using the evidence of indisputable passages to remove the
uncertainty of ambiguous ones. Here memory is extremely
valuable; and it cannot be supplied by these instructions if it is
lacking.

There are two reasons why written texts fail to be under-   32
stood: their meaning may be veiled either by unknown signs or
by ambiguous signs. Signs are either literal or metaphorical.
They are called literal when used to signify the things for
which they were invented: as, for example, when we say *bovem*
[ox], meaning the animal which we and all speakers of Latin
call by that name. They are metaphorical when the actual   33
things which we signify by the particular words are used to signify something else: when, for example, we say *bovem* and not
only interpret these two syllables to mean the animal normally
referred to by that name but also understand, by that animal,

'worker in the gospel', which is what scripture, as interpreted
by the apostle Paul, means when it says, 'You shall not muzzle
the ox that treads out the grain' [1 Cor. 9: 9 and 1 Tim. 5: 18,
quoting Deut. 25: 4].

34   An important antidote to the ignorance of literal signs is the
knowledge of languages. Users of the Latin language—and it is
these that I have now undertaken to instruct—need two
others, Hebrew and Greek, for an understanding of the divine
scriptures, so that recourse may be had to the original versions
if any uncertainty arises from the infinite variety of Latin
translators. Though we often find Hebrew words untranslated
in the texts, like *amen, alleluia, raca, hosanna* [see for example
Deut. 27: 15; Rev. 19: 1; Matt. 5: 22; John 12: 13]. In some
cases, although they could be translated, the original form is
preserved for the sake of its solemn authority (so *amen,
alleluia*); in others, like the other two that I mentioned, they are
said to be incapable of being translated into another language.

35 There are certain words in particular languages which just
cannot be translated into the idioms of another language. This
is especially true of interjections, which signify emotion rather
than an element of clearly conceived meaning: two such words,
it is said, are *raca*, a word expressing anger, and *hosanna*, a

36 word expressing joy. But it is not because of these few words,
which it is easy enough to note down and ask other people
about, but because of the aforementioned diversity of translators that a knowledge of languages is necessary. Translators of
scripture from Hebrew into Greek can be easily counted, but
not so translators into Latin, for in the early days of the faith
any person who got hold of a Greek manuscript and fancied
that he had some ability in the two languages went ahead and
translated it.

37   This fact actually proves more of a help to interpretation
than a hindrance, provided that readers are not too casual.
Obscure passages are often clarified by the inspection of several manuscripts, like the passage in Isaiah* [Isa. 58: 7] rendered by one translator as 'and do not despise the household of
your own seed', but by another as 'and do not despise your own

38 flesh'. Each one confirms the other. One is explained by the
other, because 'flesh' can be taken literally—so that one may

consider this a warning not to despise one's own body—and 'household of your seed' can be metaphorically understood as 'Christians', those spiritually born with us from the same seed of the word. But when the ideas of the translators are compared a more plausible idea suggests itself: that the command is literally about not despising your kinsfolk, since when you relate 'the household of your own seed' to the flesh your kinsfolk are what particularly comes to mind. This, I think, is the explanation of Paul's statement, 'If in any way I can arouse my flesh to jealousy, so that I may save some of them' [Rom. 11: 14] (in other words, so that they too may believe by jealously emulating those who believed earlier). By his flesh he meant the Jews, 39 by virtue of his kinship with them. Another example, again from Isaiah* [Isa. 7: 9]: one version has 'if you do not believe, you will not understand', another has 'if you do not believe, you will not stand fast'. It is not clear which of these represents the truth unless the versions in the original language are consulted. Yet both convey something important to those who read intelligently. It is difficult to find translators who diverge so much that they do not touch at some point. So because 40 understanding concerns the vision of eternal things, whereas faith nourishes us with milk, so to speak, while we are babies in the cradle of this temporal life, and because here and now 'we walk by faith, not sight' [2 Cor. 5: 7], and because if we do not walk by faith we cannot reach that vision which is not transient but eternal, and because we hold fast to the truth through a purified understanding—that is why one version says 'if you do not believe you will not stand fast' and the other 'if you do not believe you will not understand'.

Ambiguity in the original language often misleads a transla- 41 tor unfamiliar with the general sense of a passage, who may import a meaning which is quite unrelated to the writer's meaning. For example, some manuscripts have [Ps. 13: 3; cf. Rom. 3: 15 and Isa. 59: 7]: 'their feet are sharp to shed blood' (the Greek adjective means both 'sharp' and 'quick'). The translator who wrote 'their feet are quick to shed blood' saw the meaning; but another was misled by the ambiguous sign and went astray. Any other translations of this are not obscure, but 42 plain wrong. They differ from the above-mentioned examples, and our advice must be not to seek an interpretation of such texts, but an emendation. Another example: because *moschus* is 'calf' in Greek some translators did not interpret the word *moscheumata* as 'plants' but translated it as 'calves' [Wisd. 4: 3]. This mistake has taken over so many manuscripts that an alternative reading is hard to find;* and yet the meaning is quite obvious, because all is revealed in the words that follow. 'False plants do not put out deep roots' gives a better meaning here than 'calves', which are not rooted to the earth, but walk over it with their feet! This particular translation is guaranteed by the surrounding context.

43   Because the exact meaning which the various translators are trying to express, each according to his own ability and judgement, is not clear without an examination of the language being translated, and because a translator, unless very expert, often strays away from the author's meaning, we should aim either to acquire a knowledge of the languages from which the Latin scripture derives or to use the versions of those who keep excessively close to the literal meaning. Not that such translations are adequate, but they may be used to control the freedom or error of others who in their translations have chosen to

44 follow the ideas rather than the words. Translators often meet not only individual words, but also whole phrases, which simply cannot be expressed in the idioms of the Latin language, at least not if one wants to maintain the usage of ancient speakers of Latin. Sometimes these translations lose nothing in intelligibility but trouble those people who take more delight in things when correct usage is observed in expressing the corresponding signs. What is called a solecism* is simply what results when words are not combined according to the rules by which our predecessors, who spoke with some authority, combined them. Whether you say *inter homines* or *inter hominibus** does

45 not matter to a student intent upon things. And again, what is a barbarism but a word articulated with letters or sounds that are not the same as those with which it was normally articulated by those who spoke Latin before us? Whether one says *ignoscere** with a long or short third syllable is of little concern to someone who beseeches God to forgive his sins no matter how he may have managed to articulate the word.

What, then, is correctness of speech but the maintenance of the practice of others, as established by the authority of ancient speakers?

But the weaker men are, the more they are troubled by such 46 matters. Their weakness stems from a desire to appear learned, not with a knowledge of things, by which we are edified, but with a knowledge of signs, by which it is difficult not to be puffed up in some way; even a knowledge of things often makes people boastful, unless their necks are held down by the Lord's yoke. Surely there is no obstacle to the understanding in this version: 'what is the land in which they dwell upon it, whether it is good or wicked; and what are the towns in which they themselves live in them?'* [Num. 13: 19]. I judge this to be the 47 idiom of a foreign language rather than a particularly profound idea. And the version which we are now unable to remove from the mouths of our singing congregations—'over him my sanctification will flourish [*floriet*]' [Ps. 131: 18 (132: 18)]—certainly loses none of the meaning. A more educated listener would prefer it to be corrected (with *florebit* for *floriet*), and the only obstacle to this correction is the habit of those who sing it. So such matters can readily be ignored if one has no desire to avoid expressions which do not in any way detract from a sound understanding. But now take the apostolic saying, 'The 48 foolishness of God is wiser than men, and the weakness of God stronger than men' [1 Cor. 1: 25]. Suppose that someone wished to keep the Greek expression,* with *hominum* in place of *hominibus*: the mind of the alert reader would still get to the truth of the statement, but the less quick-witted reader would either fail to understand it or understand it wrongly. Such an expression is not just faulty Latin; it is potentially ambiguous, if it gives the impression that man's foolishness is wiser, and man's weakness stronger, than God's. But the alternative *sapientius est hominibus*, though free of solecism, is not free of ambiguity: it is not clear, except in the light of the context, whether 49 it is the plural of *huic homini* or *hoc homine*.* A better version would be *sapientius est quam homines* or *fortius est quam homines*.

I shall speak later about ambiguous signs; now I am dealing 50 with unfamiliar ones, of which there are two kinds, as far as words are concerned. A reader may be perplexed by either an unfamiliar word or an unfamiliar expression. If they come from other languages the information must be sought from speakers of those languages, or else the languages must be learnt (if time and ability allow), or else a collection of several translations must be consulted. If we are unfamiliar with some words and expressions in our own language, they become 51 known to us by the process of reading and listening. Nothing should be committed to memory more urgently than unfamiliar kinds of words and expressions; so that when we meet a knowledgeable person whom we can ask, or a similar expression which makes clear from the passages which precede and follow it, or both, what is the force or significance of the unfamiliar word, we can easily make a note of it, or find out about it, with the help of our memory. (Yet such is the force of habit, even in learning, that those who are nourished and educated in the holy scriptures are more surprised by expressions from elsewhere, and regard them as worse Latin than the ones which they have learnt in scripture but are not found 52 in Latin literature.) In this area too it is very helpful to collect manuscripts and examine and discuss a number of translations. But inaccuracy must be excluded, for the attention of those who wish to know the divine scripture must first focus on the task of correcting the manuscripts, so that uncorrected ones give place to corrected ones, assuming that they belong to the same type of translation.

53   Among actual translations the Itala* should be preferred to all others, as it keeps more closely to the words without sacrificing clarity of expression. To correct any Latin manuscripts Greek ones should be used: among these, as far as the Old Testament is concerned, the authority of the Septuagint is supreme. Its seventy writers are now claimed in all the more informed churches to have performed their task of translation with such strong guidance from the Holy Spirit that this great 54 number of men spoke with but a single voice.* It is generally held, and indeed asserted by many who are not unworthy of belief, that each one of these wrote his translation alone in an individual cell and nothing was found in anyone's version which was not found, in the same words and the same order of words, in the others; if so, who would dare to adapt such an

authoritative work, let alone adopt anything in preference to it? But if in fact they joined forces so as to achieve unanimity by open discussion and joint decision, even so it would not be right or proper for any one person, however expert, to think of correcting a version agreed by so many experienced scholars. Therefore, even if we find in the Hebrew versions something 55 that differs from what they wrote, I believe that we should defer to the divine dispensation which was made through them so that the books which the Jewish race refused to reveal to other peoples (whether out of religious scruple or envy) might be revealed, through the mediating power of King Ptolemy,* well in advance to the peoples that were destined to believe through our Lord. It may indeed be the case that they translated in a way that the Holy Spirit, who was leading them and creating unanimity, judged appropriate to the Gentiles. But, as 56 I said above,* the comparison of translations which have kept more closely to the words is often not without its value in explaining a passage. So, as I said to begin with, Latin manuscripts of the Old Testament should be corrected if necessary by authoritative Greek ones, and especially by the version of the scholars who though seventy in number are said to have been unanimous. The Latin manuscripts of the New Testament, if there is any uncertainty in the various Latin versions, should without doubt give place to Greek ones, especially those found in the more learned and diligent churches.

As for metaphorical signs, any unfamiliar ones which puzzle 57 the reader must be investigated partly through a knowledge of languages, and partly through a knowledge of things. There is a figurative significance and certainly some hidden meaning conveyed by the episode of the pool of Siloam [John 9: 7], where the man who had his eyes anointed by the Lord with mud made from spittle was ordered to wash his face. If the evangelist had not explained this name from an unfamiliar language, this important meaning would have remained hidden. So too, many of the Hebrew names not explained by the 58 authors of these books undoubtedly have considerable significance and much help to give in solving the mysteries of the scriptures, if they can be explained at all. Various experts in the language have rendered no small service to posterity by explaining all these individual words from the scriptures* and giving the meaning of the names Adam, Eve, Abraham, and Moses, and of place names such as Jerusalem, Zion, Jericho, Sinai, Lebanon, Jordan, and any other names in that language that are unfamiliar to us. Once these are clarified and explained many figurative expressions in scripture become quite clear.

59   Ignorance of things makes figurative expressions unclear when we are ignorant of the qualities of animals or stones or plants or other things mentioned in scripture for the sake of some analogy. The well-known fact about the snake, that it offers its whole body to assailants in place of its head, marvellously illustrates the meaning of the Lord's injunction to be as wise as serpents [Matt. 10: 16], which means that in place of our head, which is Christ [Eph. 4: 15], we should offer our body to persecutors, so that the Christian faith is not as it were

60   killed within us when we spare our body and deny God.* And the fact that a snake confined in its narrow lair puts off its old garment and is said to take on new strength* chimes in excellently with the idea of imitating the serpent's astuteness and putting off the old man (to use the words of the apostle) [Eph. 4: 22–4] in order to put on the new, and also with that of doing so in a confined place, for the Lord said 'enter by the narrow gate' [Matt. 7: 13]. Just as a knowledge of the habits of the snake clarifies the many analogies involving this animal regularly given in scripture, so too an ignorance of the numerous animals mentioned no less frequently in analogies is a great hindrance to understanding. The same is true of stones, herbs,

61   and anything that has roots. Even a knowledge of the carbuncle, a stone which shines in the dark, explains many obscure passages in scripture where it is used in an analogy; and ignorance of the beryl and adamant often closes the door to understanding. It is easy to understand that unbroken peace is signified by the olive branch brought by the dove when it returned to the ark [Gen. 8: 11], simply because we know that the smooth surface of oil is not easily broken by another liquid and also that the tree itself is in leaf all year round. And because of their ignorance about hyssop* many people, unaware of its power to cleanse the lungs or even (so it is said) to split rocks with its roots, in spite of its low and humble habit, are quite

unable to discover why it is said, 'You will purge me with hyssop, and I shall be clean' [Ps. 50: 9 (51: 7)].

An unfamiliarity with numbers makes unintelligible many 62 things that are said figuratively and mystically in scripture. An intelligent intellect (if I may put it thus) cannot fail to be intrigued by the meaning of the fact that Moses and Elijah and the Lord himself fasted for forty days [Exod. 24: 18; 3 Kgs. (1 Kgs.) 19: 8; Matt. 4: 2]. The knotty problem of the figurative significance of this event cannot be solved except by understanding and considering the number, which is four times ten, and signifies the knowledge of all things woven into the temporal order. The courses of the day and the year are based on 63 the number four: the day is divided into the hours of morning, afternoon, evening, and night, the year into the months of the spring, summer, autumn, and winter. While we live in the temporal order, we must fast and abstain from the enjoyment of what is temporal, for the sake of the eternity in which we desire to live, but it is actually the passage of time by which the lesson of despising the temporal and seeking the eternal is brought home to us. Then the number ten signifies the know- 64 ledge of the creator and creation: the Trinity is the number of the creator, while the number seven symbolizes the creation because it represents life and the body. The former has three elements (hence the precept that God must be loved with the whole heart, the whole soul, and the whole mind) [Matt. 22: 37], and as for the body, the four elements of which it consists are perfectly obvious.* To live soberly according to this significance of the number ten—conveyed to us temporally (hence the multiplication by four)—and abstain from the pleasures of this world: this is the significance of the forty-day fast. This is enjoined by the law, as represented by 65 Moses; by prophecy, as represented by Elijah; and by the Lord himself, who, to symbolize that he enjoyed the testimony of the law and the prophets, shone out in the midst of them on the mountain as the three amazed disciples looked on [Matt. 17: 1–8; Mark 9: 2–6]. In the same way a solution may be found to explain how the number fifty, which enjoys particular authority in our religion because of Pentecost,* comes from the number forty; and how, when it is multiplied by

three—either because of the three eras (before the law, under
the law, under grace) or because of the name of the Father, the
Son, and the Holy Spirit—and with the conspicuous addition
of the Trinity, refers to the mystery of the fully purified church,
matching the 153 fishes that were caught in the nets cast on the
right-hand side of the boat after the Lord's resurrection [John
21: 6–11]. In this way, expressed in a variety of numbers, there
are in the sacred books certain abstruse analogies which are
inaccessible to readers without a knowledge of number.

66   Many passages are also made inaccessible and opaque by an
ignorance of music. It has been elegantly demonstrated that
there are some figurative meanings of things based on the difference between the psaltery and the lyre.* It is a matter of dispute among experts, not unreasonably, whether the psaltery of
ten strings embodies some musical principle which obliges it
to have this number of strings, or whether, if this is not so, the
number should for that reason be understood rather in a special religious sense, either in terms of the Decalogue (and if
that number is investigated, it can only be related to the creator and the creation), or in terms of the number ten itself as
67   expounded above. The number of years given in the gospel for
the building of the Temple, forty-six [John 2: 20], has some
musical overtones, and when related to the constitution of the
Lord's body—which is why the Temple was mentioned—
compels numerous heretics to admit that the Son of God took
on a real human body, not an insubstantial one.* Indeed we
find both number and music mentioned with respect in several
68   places in the holy scriptures. But we must not listen to the fic-
tions of pagan superstition, which have represented the Muses
as the daughters of Jupiter and Memory. They were refuted
by Varro,* a man whose erudition and thirst for knowledge
could not, I think, be surpassed among pagans. He says that a
certain town (I forget its name*) placed contracts with three
workmen for three sets of images of the Muses to be set up as
an offering in Apollo's temple, intending to select and buy
69   those of the sculptor who produced the most attractive ones. It
so happened that the workmen's products were equally attractive, and the town selected all nine and they were all bought for
dedication in Apollo's temple. He adds that the poet Hesiod

later gave them names.* So Jupiter did not beget the nine
Muses, but they were made by three sculptors, three apiece.
And the town had placed contracts for three not because they   70
had seen them in a dream or because that number had
appeared before the eyes of one of its citizens, but because it
was a simple matter to observe that all sound, which is the
essence of music, is naturally threefold.* (A sound is either
produced by the voice, as by those who make music with their
mouths, without a musical instrument, or by breath, as with
trumpets and flutes, or by percussion, as in the case of lyres,
drums, or anything else which resonates when struck.) But   71
whether Varro's story is true or not, we should not avoid music
because of the associated pagan superstitions if there is a possibility of gleaning from it something of value for understanding holy scripture. Nor, on the other hand, should we be
captivated by the vanities of the theatre if we are discussing
something to do with lyres or other instruments that may help
us appreciate spiritual truths. We were not wrong to learn the   72
alphabet just because they say that the god Mercury was its
patron,* nor should we avoid justice and virtue just because
they dedicated temples to justice and virtue and preferred to
honour these values not in their minds, but in the form of
stones. A person who is a good and a true Christian should
realize that truth belongs to his Lord, wherever it is found,
gathering and acknowledging it even in pagan literature, but
rejecting superstitious vanities and deploring and avoiding
those who 'though they knew God did not glorify him as God
or give thanks but became enfeebled in their own thoughts and
plunged their senseless minds into darkness. Claiming to be
wise they became fools, and exchanged the glory of the incor-
ruptible God for the image of corruptible mortals and animals
and reptiles' [Rom. 1: 21–3].

But to analyse this whole matter more closely—and it is   73
something of the greatest importance—there are two kinds of
learning pursued even in pagan society. One consists of things
which have been instituted by humans, the other consists of
things already developed, or divinely instituted, which have
been observed by them. Of those instituted by humans, some
are superstitious, some not.

74 Something instituted by humans is superstitious if it concerns the making and worshipping of idols, or the worshipping of the created order or part of it as if it were God, or if it involves certain kinds of consultations or contracts* about meaning arranged and ratified with demons, such as the enterprises involved in the art of magic, which poets* tend to mention rather than to teach. The books of haruspices* and augurs are in this class, too—only their vanity is even more reckless.

75 To this category belong all the amulets and remedies which the medical profession also condemns, whether these consist of incantations, or certain marks which their exponents call 'characters', or the business of hanging certain things up and tying things to other things, or even somehow making things dance. The purpose of these practices is not to heal the body, but to establish certain secret or even overt meanings. They call these 'physical' matters, using this bland name to give the impression that they do not involve a person in superstition but are by nature beneficial—as, for example, earrings on the tip of one ear, or rings of ostrich bone on the fingers, or the advice given you when hiccuping to hold your left thumb with

76 your right hand. Besides all this there are thousands of utterly futile practices—do this if a part of your body suddenly twitches, do that if a stone or a dog or a slave comes between you and a friend as you walk together. The habit of treading on a stone as if it were a threat to one's friendship is less offensive than cuffing an innocent boy who happens to run between people walking together. But it is nice to record that such boys are sometimes avenged by dogs: some people are so superstitious that they go as far as striking a dog who comes between them, but they do so to their cost, because as a result of this inane remedy the dog sometimes sends its assailant straight to a real

77 doctor. Other examples are these: treading on the threshold when you pass in front of your own house; going back to bed if you sneeze while putting on your shoes; returning inside your house if you trip up while leaving it; or, when your clothing is eaten by mice, worrying more about the premonition of future disaster than about the present damage. Cato had a witty saying about this: when approached by someone who said that mice had been nibbling his slippers he replied that this was not

an omen, but would certainly have been if the slippers had been nibbling the mice.*

We must not omit from this category of deadly superstition 78 the people who are called *genethliaci* because of their study of natal days, or now in common parlance *mathematici** [astrologers]. Although they investigate the true position of the stars at a person's birth and sometimes actually succeed in working it out, the fact that they use it to try to predict our activities and the consequences of these activities is a grave error and amounts to selling uneducated people into a wretched form of slavery. When free people go to see such an 79 astrologer, they pay money for the privilege of coming away as slaves of Mars or Venus, or rather all the stars to which those who first made this error and then offered it to posterity gave either the names of animals, because they resembled animals, or the names of people, in order to honour particular people. It is no surprise that even in relatively recent times the Romans tried to consecrate the star we call Lucifer in the name of, and in honour of, Caesar.* And indeed this might have been done, 80 and become sanctified by tradition, had not Venus his ancestress, though she had never possessed it or even sought to possess it in her lifetime, already taken the name, like a piece of property, and did not transfer it in any legal way to her heirs. For when a title was vacant, and not held in the name of any previous deceased, the usual practice was followed. We call the months July and August after the human beings Julius Caesar and Augustus Caesar, and not by their old names of Quinctilis and Sextilis.* So it is easy for anyone who so wishes to understand that those planets too previously moved in the sky without their present names, but that when people died whose memory the populace was compelled by royal power, or disposed by human vanity, to honour they gave the names of the deceased to the heavenly bodies and fancied that they were raising to heaven people who as far as they themselves were concerned were dead. But whatever men may call them, the 81 heavenly bodies, which God made and arranged as he wished, certainly exist, and have fixed orbits from which the seasons derive their differences and variations. It is easy to record the details of these orbits when a person is born, according to the rules which they have invented and codified. Holy scripture condemns them when it says, 'For if they were able to know so much that they could judge the world, how is it that they did not discover its Lord more easily?' [Wisd. 13: 9].

82   But the idea of using this data to predict the character and future actions and experiences of the newborn is a great mistake, and indeed great folly. In the eyes of those who have learnt that such things are better unlearned this superstition is without the slightest doubt invalid.* (In what follows 'constellations' is their name for the diagrams of the positions occupied by the stars at the birth of the person about whom these wretched people are consulted by people even more wretched.) Now it can happen that some twins follow one another so closely out of the womb that no interval of time can be perceived between them and recorded in terms of constella-

83   tions. It follows that some twins have the same constellations, and yet their actions and experiences turn out to be not the same but often quite different.* One may live to be blissfully happy, the other to be desperately unhappy, like Esau and Jacob who, we are told, were born as twins with Jacob, the second to be born, holding in his hand the foot of his brother born

84   before him [Gen. 25: 25]. The day and hour of these births could surely have been recorded only in terms of a single constellation common to both. But the vast difference between the two in terms of character and achievement, suffering and success, is attested by scripture [Gen. 25–37] and is now com-

85   mon knowledge among all peoples. It is not pertinent to say, as they do, that the small interval, the tiny fraction of time that separates the birth of twins is of great significance in view of the nature of the universe and the great speed of the heavenly bodies. Even if I conceded that it was of the utmost significance, it would still not be discoverable by the astrologer in the constel-

86   lations from which he claims to make predictions. Since he cannot trace it in his constellations, which when examined are bound to be identical, whether he is consulted about Jacob or about his brother, what use is it to him if there is a difference in the heavens, which he thoughtlessly and casually belittles, but no difference in his diagram, which he earnestly and pointlessly beholds? So these ideas too, because they involve signs

instituted by human presumption, must be classed among those contracts and agreements made with devils.

In this way it happens that, by some inscrutable divine plan, 87 those who have a desire for evil things are handed over to be deluded and deceived according to what their own wills deserve. They are deluded and deceived by corrupt angels, to whom in God's most excellent scheme of things this lowest part of the world has been subjected by the decree of divine providence. As a result of these delusions and deceptions it has come about that these superstitious and deadly kinds of divination actually do tell of past and future things, which happen exactly as predicted; many things happen to observers in accordance with their observations, so that as they are caught up in them they become ever more inquisitive and entrap themselves more and more in the manifold snares of this most deadly error. This is a kind of spiritual fornication, 88 and in the interests of spiritual health scripture has not failed to mention it. It warned off the soul by forbidding the practice of these things, but not on the grounds that its teachers utter falsehoods; it has actually said, 'If they tell you and it happens in that way, do not trust them' [Deut. 13: 2–3]. The fact that the ghost of the dead Samuel prophesied the truth to King Saul* [1 Kgs. (1 Sam.) 28: 11–19] does not make the wickedness of summoning that ghost any less abhorrent. Nor did the fact that in Acts [Acts 16: 16–18] a soothsayer bore true testimony to the Lord's apostles lead Paul to spare that spirit rather than cleanse the woman by rebuking the demon and driving it out.

So all the specialists in this kind of futile and harmful super- 89 stition, and the contracts, as it were, of an untrustworthy and treacherous partnership established by this disastrous alliance of men and devils, must be totally rejected and avoided by the Christian. 'It is not', to quote the apostle [1 Cor. 10: 19–20], 'because an idol is something, but because whatever they sacrifice they sacrifice it to devils and not to God that I do not want you to become the associates of demons.' What the 90 apostle said about idols and the sacrifices made in their honour must guide our attitude to all these fanciful signs which draw people to the worship of idols or to the worship of the created

order or any parts of it as if they were God, or which relate to
this obsession with remedies and other such practices. They
are not publicly promulgated by God in order to foster the love
of God and one's neighbour, but they consume the hearts of
wretched mortals by fostering selfish desires for temporal
things. So in all these teachings we must fear and avoid this
alliance with demons, whose whole aim, in concert with their
leader, the devil, is to cut off and obstruct our return to God.

91 Just as there are deceptive human ideas of human origin about
the stars, which God created and ordered, so there are many
notions, apparently derived systematically from human sur-
mises and committed to paper by numerous writers, about
everything which is born or somehow comes into being by the
workings of divine providence—I mean things which happen
abnormally, like a mule giving birth or something being struck
by lightning.

92   The influence of all these things varies in proportion to the
extent of the agreement achieved with demons by presumptuous minds through such kinds of common language. But they
are all brim-full of dangerous curiosity, agonizing worry, and
deadly bondage. They were not observed as a result of their
influence, but they gained their influence as a result of being
observed and recorded. This is how they came to have different effects on different people, according to their particular
thoughts and fancies. Spirits who wish to deceive someone
devise appropriate signs for each individual to match those in
which they see him caught up through his speculations and the
93 conventions he accepts. So (by way of example) the single
letter which is written like a cross means one thing to Greeks
and another to Latin speakers, and has meaning not by nature
but by agreement and convention; therefore a person who
knows both languages does not, if he wants to say something in
writing to a Greek, write that letter with the same meaning as
it has when he writes to a Latin speaker. And the word *beta*,
consisting of the same sounds in both languages, is the name
of a letter in Greek, but a vegetable in Latin. When I say *lege*
a Greek understands one thing by these two syllables, but
94 a Latin speaker something else.* All these meanings, then,
derive their effects on the mind from each individual's

agreement with a particular convention. As this agreement
varies in extent, so do their effects. People did not agree to
use them because they were already meaningful; rather
they became meaningful because people agreed to use them.
Likewise the signs by which this deadly agreement with
demons is achieved have an effect that is in proportion to each
individual's attention to them. This is clearly demonstrated by   95
the practice of augurs, who, both before and after making
their observations, deliberately avoid seeing birds in flight or
hearing their cries, because these signs are null and void unless
accompanied by the observer's agreement.

Having pruned and uprooted these things from the Chris-   96
tian mind we must in turn consider those human institutions
which are not superstitious, that is, ones established not with
demons but with men. All things which are meaningful to
humans just because humans have decided that they should be
so are human institutions. Some of them are superfluous and
self-indulgent, others are useful and necessary. If the signs   97
made by actors while dancing were naturally meaningful,
rather than meaningful as a result of human institution and
agreement, an announcer would not have indicated to the
Carthaginians, as each actor danced, what the dance meant, as
he did in earlier days. Many old men still remember this, and
we often hear them talking about it. It is quite credible, for even
now if a person unfamiliar with these frivolities goes to the
theatre his rapt attention to them is pointless unless someone
tells him what the movements mean. Yet everyone aims at   98
some degree of similarity when they use signs, making signs as
similar as possible to the things which are signified. But
because one thing can be similar to another in many ways,
these signs are not generally understood unless accompanied
by agreement. In the case of pictures and statues and other   99
such representations, especially those made by experienced
artists, nobody who sees the representation fails to recognize
the things which they resemble. This whole category should
be classed among superfluous human institutions, except
when it makes a difference why or where or when or by whose
authority one of them is made. Finally, the thousands of
fictional stories and romances, which through their falsehoods

give people great pleasure, are human institutions. Indeed,
nothing should be thought more peculiar to mankind than
lies and falsehoods,* which derive exclusively from mankind
100 itself. But there are useful and necessary institutions, established with men by men; such things as the conventional
differences in dress and in bodily ornament, designed to
distinguish sex or rank, and countless kinds of coded meanings
without which society would function less smoothly, or not at
all, and everything in the realm of weights and measures,
coinage, and currency, which are peculiar to individual states
and peoples, and so on. If these were not human institutions
they would not differ between different peoples, nor would
they be subject to change at the whim of the authorities in each
101 country. This whole area of human institutions which con-
tribute to the necessities of life should in no way be avoided by
the Christian; indeed, within reason, they should be studied
and committed to memory.

102   There are some human institutions which are modelled on
natural ones* or at any rate similar to them. Those which
involve an alliance with demons are, as I have said, to be completely rejected and abhorred, but those which men practise
along with their fellow men are to be adopted, in so far as they
are not self-indulgent and superfluous. This applies especially to the letters of the alphabet, without which reading
would be impossible, and (up to a point) to the multiplicity of
103 languages, which I discussed above.* In this category, too, are
the symbols of shorthand, learnt by those who are now properly known as stenographers. These are useful, and it is not
wrong to learn them; they do not involve us in superstition or
undermine us with self-indulgence, provided that limited
time is spent on them and that they do not become an obstacle
to the more important things which they should help us to
obtain.

104   Now those elements of human tradition which men did not
establish but discovered by investigation, whether they were
enacted in time or instituted by God, should not be considered
human institutions, no matter where they are learnt. Some of
these concern the physical senses, others concern the mind. As
for the former, we either take them on trust when they are told

to us, or understand them when they are demonstrated, or infer them when they are experienced.

Whatever the subject called history reveals about the 105 sequence of past events is of the greatest assistance in interpreting the holy books, even if learnt outside the church as part of primary education. Many problems are often investigated by us using Olympiads and the names of consuls.* Ignorance of the consulships in which the Lord was born and died has led many to the erroneous idea that the Lord suffered at the age of 46, because it was said by the Jews that their temple (which represented the Lord's body) was built in forty-six years [John 2: 19–20]. We have it on the authority of the gospel [Luke 106 3: 23] that he was baptized at the age of about 30; the number of years that he lived after that could be inferred from the pattern of his activities, but is in fact more clearly and reliably established, beyond any shadow of doubt, by a comparison of secular history with the gospel. It will then be seen that there was some point in the statement that the Temple was built in forty-six years: since the number cannot be explained in terms of the Lord's age, it must be explained as an abstruse lesson about the human body, which the only son of God, by whom everything was made [John 1: 3], did not disdain to put on for our sake. On 107 the usefulness of history—leaving aside Greek scholars*—I cite the major problem which was solved by my good friend Ambrose. A scandalous accusation was levelled by readers and admirers of Plato, who had the nerve to say that our Lord Jesus Christ learnt all his ideas—which they cannot but marvel at and proclaim—from the works of Plato, since, undeniably, he lived long before our Lord's coming in the flesh. After examin- 108 ing secular history the aforementioned bishop discovered that Plato went to Egypt (where the prophet then was) at the time of Jeremiah,* and demonstrated that it was surely more likely that Plato had been introduced to our literature by Jeremiah, and that it was this that enabled him to learn and write the things for which he is justly praised. In fact the literature of the Hebrew race, in which monotheism first made its appearance, and from which our Lord came according to the flesh [Rom. 9: 5], was not preceded even by Pythagoras,* from whose followers they claim that Plato learnt his theology. So as a result of studying the chronology it is much easier to believe that the pagans took everything that is good and true in their writings from our literature than that the Lord Jesus Christ took his from Plato—a quite crazy idea.

109　　Historical narrative also describes human institutions of the past, but it should not for that reason itself be counted among human institutions. For what has already gone into the past and cannot be undone must be considered part of the history of time, whose creator and controller is God. There is a difference between describing what has been done and describing what must be done. History relates past events in a faithful and useful way, whereas the books of haruspices and similar literature set out to teach things to be performed or observed, and offer impertinent advice, not reliable information.

110　　There is also a kind of narration akin to demonstration, by which things in the present, and not the past, are communicated to people unfamiliar with them. In this category are various studies of topography and zoology, and of trees, plants, stones, and other such things. I dealt with this category earlier* and explained that such knowledge is valuable in solving puzzles in scripture, but is not to be used in place of certain signs to provide the remedies or devices associated with some superstition. I distinguished this category too from the one that is lawful and open to Christians. For it is one thing to say, 'if you drink this plant in powdered form your stomach will stop hurting', and another to say, 'if you hang this plant round your neck your stomach will stop hurting'. In the one case the health-giving mixture is commendable, in the other the superstitious meaning

111　　is damnable. But in the absence of incantations or invocations or 'characters'* it is often doubtful whether the thing tied on or attached in some way for healing the body works by nature—in which case it may be used freely—or succeeds by virtue of some meaningful association; in this case, the more effectively it appears to heal, the more a Christian should be on guard. Where the explanation of its power is not apparent, it is the attitude of the user that matters, as far as physical healing or treatment, whether in medicine or in agriculture, is concerned.

112　　In astronomy—scripture mentions just a few things here— we have a case not of narration but demonstration. The orbit of

the moon, which is regularly used to fix the annual celebration
of our Lord's passion, is familiar to very many people, but very
few have infallible knowledge about the rising or setting or any
other movements of the other heavenly bodies. In itself, this 113
knowledge, although not implicating one in superstition, does
not give much help in interpreting the divine scripture—
almost none, in fact—and is really more of a hindrance, since it
demands the fruitless expenditure of effort. Because it is akin
to the deadly error of those who prophesy fatuously about fate,
it is more convenient and honourable to despise it. But as well
as the demonstration of things in the present it has something
in common with narration of the past, because one may
systematically argue from the present position and movement
of the stars to their courses in the past. It also makes possible
systematic predictions about the future, which are not speculative and conjectural but firm and certain; but we should not
try to extract something of relevance to our own actions
and experiences, like the maniacs who cast horoscopes, but
confine our interest to the stars themselves. Just as someone 114
who studies the moon can say, after examining how large it is
today, how large it was so many years ago or how large it will be
in so many years' time, so in the same way skilled astronomers
have learnt to pronounce about each of the stars. I have now
explained my position on this whole subject, as far as its
practical uses are concerned.

In the case of the other arts, by which something is manu- 115
factured, whether it be an artefact that remains after a crafts-
man has worked on it, like a house or a stool or a vessel of some
kind, and so on, or whether they provide some service for God
to work with, like medicine, agriculture, or navigation, or
whether the whole end-product consists in action, as in dancing, running, and wrestling—in all these arts knowledge
gained from past experiences causes future ones to be inferred.
None of these craftsmen moves a muscle at his work except to
link his experience of the past with his plans for the future. In 116
human life knowledge of these things is to be used sparingly
and in passing, and not in order to make things—unless a particular task demands it, which is not my concern now—but to
assist our judgement, so that we are not entirely unaware of

what scripture wishes to convey when it includes figurative
expressions based on these arts.

117   That leaves subjects which concern not the physical senses
but mental reasoning. Dominant here are the subjects of logic
and number, but logic is of paramount importance in understanding and resolving all kinds of problems in the sacred
texts. But one must beware of indulging a passion for wrangling and making a puerile show of skill in trapping an opponent. There are many 'sophisms', as they are called, or invalid
deductions, framed as a rule in the guise of valid ones, designed
to trap not just dull people but also clever ones who are less
118   than consistently alert. The following proposition was put by
X to Y: 'you are not what I am'. Y agreed; that was, after all,
true up to a point, or else Y was just being simple-minded
because of X's deviousness. X added, 'I am a man', and when
Y granted this too, he concluded 'therefore you are not a man'.
This kind of captious argument is, in my opinion, deplored by
scripture in the passage where it says 'The person who speaks
sophistically is odious' [Ecclus. 37: 23]. (But the word 'sophis-
tical' is also applied to a style which is not captious, but goes in
for verbal ornament on a scale that does not suit a serious
writer.)

119   There are also such things as valid logical syllogisms based
on false statements, which attack a mistake made by an opponent. But these are advanced by honest and clever people to
embarrass the person whom they are seeking to attack and
make him abandon his misconception, by showing that if he
chooses to stick to it he is logically compelled to uphold what
he condemns. The apostle Paul was not advancing true statements* when he said [1 Cor. 15: 13–14], 'neither did Christ
rise', and 'our preaching is in vain', and 'your faith is in vain',
and then other things, which are completely false; because
Christ did rise, and the preaching of those who reported this
was not in vain, nor was the faith of those who had believed it.
But these falsehoods were deduced quite validly from the
120   proposition that there is no resurrection of the dead. Because
these propositions are true if it is the case that the dead do
not rise, the resurrection of the dead will follow when these
falsehoods are refuted. There are, then, valid syllogisms based

not only on true propositions but also on false ones; it is easy to learn which of them are valid even in schools outside the church. But the truth of propositions must be sought in the church's holy books.

The validity of syllogisms is not something instituted by 121 humans, but observed and recorded by them, so that the subject may be taught or learnt. It is built into the permanent and divinely instituted system of things. The historian does not himself produce the sequence of events which he narrates, and the writer on topography or zoology or roots or stones does not present things instituted by humans, and the astronomer who points out the heavenly bodies and their movements does not point out something instituted by himself or any other person; likewise the logician who says 'since the consequent is false, the antecedent must be false' may be saying something perfectly true, but does not himself make it true, for he only points out the truth of it. The above-quoted text of Paul is an 122 instance of this rule; for the antecedent was that there was no resurrection of the dead, as claimed by those whose error the apostle wanted to demolish. From that antecedent, by which they maintained that there was no resurrection of the dead, the statement 'nor did Christ rise' logically follows. But that conclusion is false, since Christ did rise; so the antecedent too is false. The antecedent was that there is no resurrection of the dead; therefore there is a resurrection of the dead. All of which 123 may be put briefly like this: if there is no resurrection of the dead, Christ did not rise either; but Christ did rise, so there is a resurrection of the dead. This fact, then—that by refuting the consequent you necessarily refute the antecedent too—was not instituted but pointed out by man. This rule relates to the validity of deductions, and not to the truth of propositions.

But in this last statement about the resurrection, the logical 124 deduction was valid, and the actual proposition expressed in the conclusion was true. There may, however, be a valid deduction using false propositions, as in the following example. Suppose someone granted that if a snail is an animal, it has a voice. With this granted, it is then shown that a snail does not have a voice, and the deduction made—because when a conclusion is refuted the antecedent is also refuted—that a

snail is not an animal. This proposition is false, but validly
125 derived from the false premiss that was granted. So whereas
the truth of a proposition holds good through itself alone, the
truth-value of a syllogistic conclusion is established from
what the disputant believes or concedes. This explains why,
as I said before, a falsehood is inferred in a valid process of
reasoning to make the person whose error we wish to correct
ashamed to have held opinions with consequences that he can
see must be rejected. It is now easy to understand that there can
be invalid deductions from true statements, just as there are
valid ones from false statements. Suppose that someone put
the proposition, 'if X is just, he is good', and that this was
granted; that he then said, 'but X is not just'; and then, with
126 that granted, added the conclusion 'so X is not good'. Even if
all these statements were true, the deduction is not valid. For
although it is necessarily the case that an antecedent is refuted
by the refutation of the consequent, it is not the case that a
consequent is refuted by the refutation of an antecedent. It is
correct to say 'if he is an orator, he is a man', but if you then add
the minor premiss, 'he is not an orator', it will not follow that
'he is not therefore a man'.

127   So knowing the rules of valid deduction is not the same
thing as knowing the truth of propositions. In logic one learns
about valid and invalid inference, and contradiction. A valid
inference is 'if he is an orator he is a man'; an invalid one is 'if
he is a man, he is an orator'; a contradictory one is 'if he is a
man, he is a quadruped'. In these cases a judgement is made
about the actual deduction. On the other hand, where the truth
of propositions is concerned, it is the actual propositions in
themselves, not their logical relationships, that need to be
examined. But when uncertain propositions are combined
with true and certain ones in a valid process of reasoning, it
128 necessarily follows that they too become certain. Some people
give themselves airs when they have learnt the rules of valid
deduction, as if the truth of propositions resided in that. And
conversely some people, although they often hold a true
opinion, wrongly despise themselves for being ignorant of the
laws of inference, although it is better to know that there
is a resurrection of the dead than to know that if there is no

resurrection of the dead it necessarily follows that Christ did not rise either.

The study of definition, division, and classification, though 129
often applied to false things, is not in itself false; and it was not instituted by man, but discovered as part of the way things are. For just because it is often applied by poets to their fables and by false philosophers or heretics (in other words, false Christians) to the tenets of their misguided systems, that does not make it wrong to say that in defining or dividing or classifying something you must not include something irrelevant or leave out something that is relevant. This is true, even if the things being defined or classified are not true. Falsehood itself can be 130
defined—we might say that falsehood is the description of something which is not actually in the state in which it is asserted to be, or put it in some other way—and the definition may be correct, although what is false cannot be true. We may also subdivide it, saying that there are two kinds of falsehood, one consisting of things which cannot possibly be true, another of things which are not true, but could be. If you say that seven 131
and three make eleven, you are saying something that cannot possibly be true, but if you say, for example, that it rained on New Year's Day, although in fact it did not, you are saying something which could have been true. So the definition and subdivision of falsehoods may be perfectly correct, although the falsehoods themselves are certainly not true.

There are also certain rules of the more flamboyant 132
discipline now called eloquence,* which are valid in spite of the fact that they can be used to commend falsehood. Since they can also be used to commend the truth, it is not the subject itself that is reprehensible, but the perversity of those who abuse it. It is not the result of human institution that the expression of love* wins over one's listeners, or that a brief and lucid narrative communicates facts efficiently, or that variety holds the attention without creating boredom; these and other such observations are true whether applied to true matters or false, to the extent that they cause something to be known or believed, or influence minds to seek or to avoid something. It was discovered that these things were true, not decided that they should be true. But when this subject is learnt, it has to be 133

used in communicating what has already been understood
rather than in the actual process of understanding. The rules
about syllogisms and definitions and classifications, on the
other hand, greatly help people to understand, provided that
they avoid the error of thinking that when they have mastered
134 them they have learnt the actual truth about the happy life. But
it tends to be the case that people develop the skills which the
learning of these details is meant to develop more easily than
they pick up the tortuous and rebarbative lessons of their
teachers. It is as if someone who wanted to give rules about
walking were to tell you that your back foot should not be
raised until you have put down your front foot, and then
describe in minute detail how you should move the joints of
your limbs and knees. He would be right; walking in any other
way is impossible. But people find it easier to walk by actually
doing these things than by paying attention to them as they do
135 them or by assimilating rules when they hear them. Those who
are unable to walk pay much less heed to instructions which
they cannot follow in practice. Similarly, a clever person is
as a rule quicker to see that a conclusion is invalid than to
understand the relevant rules; the dull person fails to see it, but
has even less chance of understanding the rules. In all these
matters it is often true that the pleasure derived from the open
display of truth is greater than the assistance gained from
discussing or examining it, though indeed these things can
sharpen the intellect, which is a good thing provided that they
do not also make people more mischievous or conceited or, in
other words, more inclined to deceive others by plausible
talk and questioning, or to think that by learning these things
they have done something marvellous which entitles them to
consider themselves superior to ordinary unsophisticated
people.
136   As for the study of number, it is surely clear even to the
dullest person that it was not instituted by men, but rather
investigated and discovered. Virgil wanted the first vowel of
Italia—traditionally pronounced short—to be long, and made
it long;* but nobody can bring it about by willing it that three
threes are not nine, or that they fail to make a squared number,
or that the number nine is not thrice three, or one and a half

times six, or twice no number (for odd numbers are not divisible by two*). So whether numbers are considered purely as   137
numbers or used in accordance with the laws that govern
figures or sounds or other kinds of motion, they have fixed
rules, which were not in any way instituted by human beings
but discovered by the intelligence of human brains.

Some people take such delight in all this that they like to   138
boast among the unlearned instead of asking why the things
which they simply perceive to be true actually are true, or why
things that are not only true but also unchangeable (as they
have understood them to be) actually are unchangeable; nor do
they, as they come from the visible and physical to the human
mind and find this too to be changeable—because it is now
clever, now not,* being placed between the unchangeable
truth above them and the changeable things below them—
relate all these things to the praise and love of God, realizing
that it is from him that all things have their existence. Such
people may seem learned, but are in no way wise.

So it seems to me that the following advice is beneficial for   139
young people who are keen and intelligent, who fear God and
seek a life of true happiness. Do not venture without due care
into any branches of learning which are pursued outside the
church of Christ, as if they were a means to attaining the happy
life, but discriminate sensibly and carefully between them.
Those that are found to be of human institution—these come
in many forms, because of the many different aims of those
who instituted them, but offer little certainty, because of the
speculative ideas of fallible people which underlie them—
should be entirely repudiated and treated with disgust,
especially if they involve an alliance with demonic powers
established through a sort of contract or agreement to use
particular esoteric meanings. Keep away too from the unnecessary and self-indulgent institutions of mankind, but in
view of the demands of this present life do not neglect the
human institutions vital to the cohesion of society. As for the   140
other branches of learning found in pagan society, apart from
the study of things past or present which concern the bodily
senses (including the productions and experimentations of the
practical arts) and the sciences of logic and number,* I consider

nothing useful here. In all these subjects the watchword must be 'nothing in excess',* and nowhere more so than in those which concern the bodily senses and are subject to time or
141 restricted in space. Some scholars have made separate studies of all the words and names in Hebrew, Syriac, Egyptian, or any other language found in the holy scriptures that are used without any interpretation;* and Eusebius made a separate study of chronology,* because of the problems in the divine books which require its application. They did this in these specialized areas to save the Christian student a lot of bother over a few details. In the same way I can see the possibility that if someone suitably qualified were interested in devoting a generous amount of time to the good of his brethren he could compile a monograph classifying and setting out all the places, animals, plants, and trees, or the stones and metals, and all the
142 other unfamiliar kinds of object mentioned in scripture. It might also be possible to put together an explanatory account of numbers, confined to numbers mentioned in the divine scripture. Perhaps indeed some or all of this has already been done; I have come across much information on which I did not realize that good and learned Christians had done research or written books. These things tend to remain unknown, whether because the bulk of scholars neglect them, or because jealous
143 ones conceal them.* Whether the same can be done for logic, I do not know. I rather think not, because logic permeates the whole body of scripture, rather like a network of muscles, and so is of more help to the reader in resolving and revealing ambiguities—of which I will speak later*—than in understanding unfamiliar signs, which is my present concern.
144   Any statements by those who are called philosophers, especially the Platonists,* which happen to be true and consistent with our faith should not cause alarm, but be claimed for our own use, as it were from owners who have no right to them. Like the treasures of the ancient Egyptians, who possessed not only idols and heavy burdens, which the people of Israel hated and shunned, but also vessels and ornaments of silver and gold, and clothes, which on leaving Egypt the people of Israel, in order to make better use of them, surreptitiously claimed for themselves (they did this not on their own authority but at

God's command, and the Egyptians in their ignorance actually gave them the things of which they had made poor use*) [Exod. 3: 21–2, 12: 35–6]—similarly all the branches of pagan 145 learning contain not only false and superstitious fantasies and burdensome studies* that involve unnecessary effort, which each one of us must loathe and avoid as under Christ's guidance we abandon the company of pagans, but also studies for liberated minds which are more appropriate to the service of the truth, and some very useful moral instruction, as well as the various truths about monotheism to be found in their writers. These treasures—like the silver and gold, which they did not create but dug, as it were, from the mines of providence, which is everywhere—which were used wickedly and harmfully in the service of demons must be removed by Christians, as they separate themselves in spirit from the wretched company of pagans, and applied to their true function, that of preaching the gospel. As for their clothing—which corresponds to human institutions, but those appropriate to human society, which in this life we cannot do without—this may be accepted and kept for conversion to Christian purposes. This is exactly 146 what many good and faithful Christians have done. We can see, can we not, the amount of gold, silver, and clothing with which Cyprian, that most attractive writer and most blessed martyr, was laden when he left Egypt; is not the same true of Lactantius, and Victorinus, of Optatus, and Hilary,* to say nothing of people still alive,* and countless Greek scholars? Isn't this what had been done earlier by Moses himself, that most faithful servant of God, of whom it is written that he was trained in all the wisdom of the Egyptians [Acts 7: 22]? Pagan 147 society, riddled with superstition, would never have given to all these men the arts which it considered useful—least of all at a time when it was trying to shake off the yoke of Christ and persecuting Christians—if it had suspected that they would be adapted to the purpose of worshipping the one God, by whom the worship of idols would be eradicated. But they did give their gold and silver and clothing to God's people as it left Egypt, little knowing that the things they were giving away would be put back into the service of Christ. The event narrated in Exodus was certainly a figure, and this is what it foreshadowed. (I say this without prejudice to any other interpretation of equal or greater importance.)

148　　As students of the divine scriptures, equipped in this way, begin to approach the task of studying them in detail, they must ponder incessantly this phrase of the apostle Paul: 'knowledge puffs up, but love builds up' [1 Cor. 8: 1]. In this way, even if they leave Egypt well provided for, they realize that without first observing the Passover they cannot be saved. Now 'Christ our Passover has been sacrificed' [1 Cor. 5: 7]; the sacrifice of Christ teaches us nothing more clearly than what he himself calls out, as if to those whom he sees suffering in Egypt under Pharaoh: 'Come unto me, you who labour and are heavy laden, and I will refresh you. Take my yoke upon you and learn from me, for I am gentle and lowly in heart, and you will find rest for your souls. My yoke is a soft one, and my burden light' [Matt. 11: 28–30]. Who are these if not the gentle and lowly in heart, people not puffed up by knowledge but built up by love?

149　　Remember those who celebrated the Passover in days gone by, in its unreal and shadowy form; when the command was given to mark their gateposts with the blood of a lamb, they were also sprinkled with hyssop [Exod. 12: 22]. This is a lowly and gentle plant, but nothing is stronger or more penetrating than its roots, so that 'rooted and grounded in love' we may be able 'to comprehend with all the saints what is the breadth and length and height and depth'* [Eph. 3: 18]. This refers to the Lord's cross. The breadth is the crossbeam, on which the hands were stretched out; the length is the part from the ground to the crossbeam, to which is fixed the whole body from the hands downward; the height is the part from the crossbeam up to the top, to which the head is attached; the

150　　depth is the hidden part, firmly set in the ground. In the symbol of the cross every Christian act is inscribed: to do good in Christ and to hold fast resolutely to him, to hope for heaven, to avoid profaning the sacraments. If we are purified by such behaviour we will be able 'to know the love of Christ which surpasses knowledge' [Eph. 3: 19]—the love in which he, by whom everything was made [John 1: 3], is equal to the Father—and so be filled with all the fullness of God. Hyssop also has a cleansing power, so that nobody should boast, with his head inflated* by a knowledge of the wealth he has taken from Egypt. 'You will sprinkle me with hyssop,' Scripture says, 'and I shall be made clean; you will wash me, and I shall be whiter than snow. You will give exultation and joy to my ears' [Ps. 50: 9–10 (51: 7–8)]. Then to follow that up it adds, to demonstrate that hyssop signifies cleansing from pride: 'the bones once abased will rejoice'.

The insignificance of the amount of gold, silver, and clothing which that people took away with it from Egypt, in comparison with the wealth that it later attained in Jerusalem, as shown particularly in the reign of Solomon [3 Kgs. (1 Kgs.) 10: 14–27], is the measure of the insignificance of all knowledge, I mean useful knowledge, that is collected from pagan books, when compared with the knowledge contained in the divine scriptures. For what a person learns independently of scripture is condemned there if it is harmful, but found there if it is useful. And when one has found there all the useful knowledge that can be learnt anywhere else, one will also find there, in much greater abundance, things which are learnt nowhere else at all, but solely in the remarkable sublimity and the remarkable humility of the scriptures. Readers furnished with such an education will not be held back by unfamiliar signs. Gentle and lowly in heart, peacefully subject to Christ, laden with a light burden, founded and rooted and built up in love, and incapable of being puffed up by knowledge, they should now proceed to consider and analyse the ambiguous signs in the scriptures, about which I will now endeavour to present, in my third book, such learning as the Lord deigns to deliver to me.

BOOK THREE

1 The student who fears God earnestly seeks his will in the holy scriptures. Holiness makes him gentle, so that he does not revel in controversy; a knowledge of languages protects him from uncertainty over unfamiliar words or phrases, and a knowledge of certain essential things protects him from ignorance of the significance and detail of what is used by way of imagery. Thus equipped, and with the assistance of reliable texts derived from the manuscripts with careful attention to the need for emendation,* he should now approach the task of

2 analysing and resolving the ambiguities of the scriptures. To prevent himself from being misled by ambiguous signs, in so far as I can instruct him (it may indeed be the case that either because of great intellectual gifts or a clarity of mind that is the result of greater illumination than I have he scorns as elementary the methods which I wish to demonstrate)—but, as I began to say, in so far as I can instruct him, the student who is in the proper state of mind to accept my instruction should know that ambiguity in scripture resides either in literal or in metaphorical usages (as the terms were described in Book 2).*

3 When it is literal usages that make scripture ambiguous, we must first of all make sure that we have not punctuated or articulated the passage incorrectly. Once close consideration has revealed that it is uncertain how a passage should be punctuated and articulated,* we must consult the rule of faith,* as it is perceived through the plainer passages of the scriptures and the authority of the church. (I dealt adequately with this mat-

4 ter when speaking of things in Book 1.) But if both interpretations, or indeed all of them, if there are several sides to the ambiguity, sound compatible with the faith, then it remains to consult the context—the preceding and following passages, which surround the ambiguity—in order to determine which of the several meanings that suggest themselves is supported by it, and which one lends itself to acceptable combinations with it.

5 Consider now the following examples. The well-known

heretical punctuation* 'In the beginning was the Word, and
the Word was with God, and there was God' [John 1: 1–2], giving a different sense in what follows ('This Word was in the
beginning with God') refuses to acknowledge that the Word
was God. This is to be refuted by the rule of faith, which lays
down for us the equality of the members of the Trinity, and so
we should say 'and the Word was God', and then go on, 'This
was in the beginning with God.' The following ambiguous 6
passage is not, on either interpretation, at odds with the faith,
and therefore has to be resolved by its actual context. The
apostle says, 'And I know not which to choose; I am torn in two
directions having a desire to be dissolved and be with Christ,
for that is much the best; to remain in the flesh is necessary on
your account'* [Phil. 1. 22–4]. It is not in fact clear whether we
should read 'having a desire in two directions' or 'I am torn in
two directions', followed by 'having a desire to be dissolved
and be with Christ'. But since the phrase 'for that is much the 7
best' follows, it is clear that he says he has a desire for that
which is best, so that although torn in two directions he feels a
desire to do the one but an obligation to do the other (that is, a
desire to be with Christ, but an obligation to remain in the
flesh). The ambiguity is resolved by the presence of the single
word 'for'. Critics who remove this word have been led to the
conclusion that he was apparently not only torn in two directions but also had a desire for two things.* So the punctuation 8
must be: 'and I know not which to choose; I am torn in two
directions' (pause) 'having a desire to be dissolved and be with
Christ'. And then, as if he were being asked why he has a desire
for this, he says, 'for it is much the best'. Why, then, is he torn
in two directions? Because there is an obligation to remain,
which he expresses thus: 'to remain in the flesh is necessary on
your account'. Where an ambiguity can be resolved neither by 9
an article of faith nor by the actual context there is no objection
to any punctuation which follows one of the meanings that
suggest themselves. Such is the passage in Corinthians: 'so
having these promises, my dearest brethren, let us purify ourselves from all pollution of the flesh and the spirit, perfecting
holiness in the fear of God. Welcome me; I have wronged no
one'* [2 Cor. 7: 1–2]. It is uncertain whether we should read

'let us purify ourselves from all pollution of the flesh and the
spirit', on the analogy of the phrase 'so that she may be holy in
body and spirit' [1 Cor. 7: 34], or 'let us purify ourselves from
all pollution of the flesh', with a different sense emerging in
what follows: 'and perfecting holiness of the spirit in the fear of
God. Welcome me . . .' Such problems of punctuation are for
the reader to resolve.

10   The points that I have just made about problems of punctuation also apply to the problems of reading aloud. These too,
unless they are simply mistakes due to a reader's gross care-
lessness, are resolved by considering either the rules of faith or
the surrounding context. If neither of these methods is used to
resolve them they will none the less remain in dispute, but in
such a way that the reader will not be wrong however the pas-
11   sages are articulated. If our faith did not prevent it—for we
believe that God will not make accusations against his elect and
that Christ will not condemn the elect—the following passage
might be read in such a way that the question, 'Who will make
an accusation against God's elect?' [Rom. 8: 33–4], is followed
by a sort of answer in the words 'God who justifies them', and
then, similarly, by the question, 'Who is it that condemns
them?', and the answer, 'Christ Jesus who died'. But since it
would be crazy to believe this, it will be articulated as a *percon-*
12   *tatio* followed by an *interrogatio*. (The difference between
these, according to ancient authorities,* is that many answers
may be given to the former, but only 'yes' and 'no' to the latter.)
So it will be articulated in such a way that what follows the *per-*
contatio ('Who will make an accusation against God's elect?') is
intoned interrogatively ('God who justifies them?'), expecting
the tacit answer 'no'; and this is followed similarly by a *percon-*
tatio ('Who is it that condemns?'), and another *interrogatio*
('Christ Jesus who died, but who rose again, who is at God's
right hand, and who pleads for us?'), all of them expecting the
13   tacit answer 'no'. But in the passage where he says 'What shall
we say then? That the Gentiles, who did not pursue righteousness, attained righteousness' [Rom. 9: 30], the text that follows
will not make sense unless the question 'What shall we say
then?' is followed by the reply 'That the Gentiles, who did not
pursue righteousness, attained righteousness'. But I fail to see

how to determine with what tone Nathaniel's words *a Nazareth potest aliquid boni esse* [John 1: 46] should be articulated— whether they should be read as a statement with only the words *a Nazareth* forming a question, or read entirely with the hesitant tone of a question.* Neither interpretation is contrary to the faith.

Ambiguity is also present where the length of syllables is   14 uncertain; and this too of course is relevant to reading aloud. In the sentence *Non est absconditum a te os meum, quod fecisti in abscondito** [Ps. 138: 15 (139: 15)] it is not obvious as one reads whether one should pronounce *os* with a short or long vowel. If it is made short, the singular of the word *ossa* [bone] is understood; if long, the singular of *ora* [mouth]. Such matters are   15 settled by an inspection of the original: in Greek the word denotes not 'mouth', but 'bone'. So the colloquial manner of speaking is often more effective than the propriety of literary language when it comes to signifying things. Indeed, I would prefer the sentence *Non est absconditum a te ossum meum*, which includes a barbarism,* to one which because it is better Latin is less clear. Sometimes such doubts about the length of a syllable may be resolved by a nearby word which is relevant to the meaning, as in the sentence of the apostle Paul, *Quae praedico vobis sicut praedixi, quoniam qui talia agunt regnum dei non possidebunt** [Gal. 5: 21]. If he had said simply *Quae praedico vobis*, without adding *sicut praedixi*, it would be necessary to   16 refer to a manuscript in the original language to find out whether to pronounce the middle syllable of the word *praedico* long or short.* But in this case it is clear that it should be long; he said not *sicut praedicavi* but *sicut praedixi*. As well as these ambiguities we must consider in a similar way those   17 which do not concern punctuation or reading aloud, like the one in Thessalonians' *Propterea consolati sumus fratres in vobis* [1 Thess. 3: 7]. It is not clear whether *fratres* is in the vocative case or the accusative; neither reading would be contrary to the faith. But in Greek the corresponding case-forms are not identical, and so after inspecting the Greek we declare in favour of the vocative (equivalent to *o fratres*). If a translator   18 had chosen to say *Propterea consolationem habuimus, fratres, in vobis*, he would have been less faithful to the wording, but there

would be no doubt of his meaning. Or indeed *nostri* might be added, for hardly anyone would doubt that the vocative was being used in the phrase *Propterea consolati sumus fratres nostri in vobis*. But it is rather dangerous to allow such changes. This has been done in Corinthians [1 Cor. 15: 31], where the apostle says *cotidie morior, per vestram gloriam, fratres, quam habeo in Christo*
19 *Iesu*: one translator actually wrote *cotidie morior, per vestram iuro gloriam*, because in Greek there is a clear and unambiguous word signifying an oath.* In the field of literal expressions, then, as far as the books of holy scripture are concerned, it is very unusual, and very difficult, to find cases of ambiguity which cannot be resolved either by the particular details of the context—which are a pointer to the writer's intention—or by a comparison of Latin translations or an inspection of the original language.

20   But the ambiguities of metaphorical words, about which I must now speak, require no ordinary care and attention. To begin with, one must take care not to interpret a figurative expression literally. What the apostle says is relevant here: 'the letter kills but the spirit gives life' [2 Cor. 3: 6]. For when something meant figuratively is interpreted as if it were meant literally, it is understood in a carnal way. No 'death of the soul' is more aptly given that name than the situation in which the intelligence, which is what raises the soul above the level of ani-
21 mals, is subjected to the flesh by following the letter. A person who follows the letter understands metaphorical words as literal, and does not relate what the literal word signifies to any other meaning. On hearing the word 'sabbath', for example, he interprets it simply as one of the seven days which repeat themselves in a continuous cycle; and on hearing the word 'sacrifice' his thoughts do not pass beyond the rituals performed with sacrificial beasts or fruits of the earth. It is, then, a miserable kind of spiritual slavery to interpret signs as things, and to be incapable of raising the mind's eye above the physical creation so as to absorb the eternal light.

22   But the form this slavery took in the Jewish people was very different from the experience of other nations, since notwithstanding their enslavement to temporal things the idea of monotheism was presented to them in all sorts of ways. And

although they observed the signs of spiritual things in place of
the things themselves—not knowing what they related to—
they nevertheless had an ingrained belief that such slavery
made them acceptable to the single God of all, the God whom
they were unable to see. This relationship, as the apostle Paul
wrote [Gal. 3: 24], was like the protection of children by a
pedagogue.* That is why the people who resolutely held fast to   23
these signs were unable, when the time had come for them to
be explained, to tolerate the Lord who disregarded them; and
that is why their leaders engineered false accusations against
him because he healed on the sabbath [Matt. 12: 1–14; Luke 6:
1–11], and why the people, devoted to signs as if they were
things, did not believe that he was God or that he had come
from God, since he refused to follow these practices in the way
that they were observed by the Jews. But those who did
believe, those who became the first church of Jerusalem,
clearly showed what an advantage it was to have had the protection of a pedagogue in this way; for the result was that the
signs temporarily imposed on them in their slavery drew the
thoughts of those who observed them to the worship of the one
God who created heaven and earth. Because they were very   24
close to being spiritual—for although they did not know how
to interpret them spiritually, the vows and signs concerned
with the world and the flesh had at least taught them to worship
the one eternal God—they were so receptive to the Holy Spirit
that they sold all their possessions and placed the proceeds at
the apostles' feet for distribution to the poor, dedicating themselves wholly to God [Acts 4: 32–5]. And so they formed a new
temple, a temple whose earthly counterpart they had served
previously. It is not recorded that any Gentile churches did   25
this; for those who thought of manufactured statues as gods
were not found to be so spiritually aware. If any of them ever   26
did try to interpret these statues as signs, they related them to
the worship and veneration of the created order. For what
good is it, I ask, that (for example) an image of Neptune is not
thought of as a god in itself, but considered to represent the
whole sea or all the other kinds of watercourse that flow from
springs? He is so described by one of their poets, if I remember
rightly, in these words:

Thou, father Neptune, whose hoary temples resound to the splash of
the encircling sea, from whose mighty chin flows the great ocean, in
whose hair rivers meander . . .*

27   Inside its attractive shell this husk is a jangle of fine-sounding
stones; but it is the food of pigs, not men. (Anyone who knows
the gospel knows my meaning.*) What good is it then, I ask,
that a representation of Neptune is given this significance,
except perhaps to make me avoid both kinds of worship? As far
as I am concerned, any statue is as far from being God as the
whole sea is. I admit, however, that those who regard the works
of men as gods are more bogged down in error than those who
so regard the works of God. But we are instructed to love and
worship the one God who created all these things of which they
venerate images, whether they do so by treating them as gods

28   or as signs or representations of gods. If, then, it is a carnal
form of slavery to follow a sign divinely instituted for a useful
purpose instead of the thing that it was instituted to represent,
is it not far worse to accept as things the humanly instituted
signs of useless things? If you relate such signs to the actual
things signified by them, and commit your soul to worshipping
them, you will still not be free from the oppression and the
delusion of this servile and carnal condition.

29   So Christian freedom has liberated those whom it found
enslaved to useful signs—they were, so to speak, not that far
away—and by interpreting the signs to which they were subjected has raised them to the level of the things of which these
were signs. These people formed the churches of the holy
Israelites. But as for those whom it found under the influence
of useless signs, it has undermined not only their servile attention to such signs, but also the signs themselves; and it has
eliminated them all, so that the Gentiles might turn away from
the pollution of a horde of fictitious gods—something which
scripture frequently, and literally, calls fornication—to the
worship of a single god, and no longer live in slavery, even to
useful signs, but rather exercise their minds by the discipline

30   of understanding them spiritually. Someone who attends to
and worships a thing which is meaningful but remains unaware
of its meaning is a slave to a sign. But the person who attends to
or worships a useful sign, one divinely instituted, and does

realize its force and significance, does not worship a thing which is only apparent and transitory but rather the thing to which all such things are to be related. Such a person is spiritual and free—and this was true even in the era of slavery when the time was not yet ripe for carnal minds to receive the clarification of the signs by which they had to be disciplined, like oxen beneath a yoke. Among such spiritual people were 31 the patriarchs and prophets and all those in the people of Israel through whom the Holy Spirit provided us with the support and comfort of the scriptures. But at the present time, when a brilliant demonstration of our freedom has been revealed in the resurrection of our Lord, we are not oppressed by the tiresome necessity of attending to signs, even the signs which we now understand. Instead of many signs there are now but a few signs, simple when performed, inspiring when understood, and holy when practised, given to us by the teaching of our Lord himself and the apostles, such as the sacrament of baptism and the celebration of the Lord's body and blood. When 32 an individual understands these, he recognizes with an inner knowledge what they relate to, and consequently venerates them not because of any carnal slavery but because of his spiritual freedom. And just as it is a mark of servile weakness to follow the letter and accept the signs rather than the things signified by them, so it is a mark of badly misguided error to interpret signs in a useless way. The person who does not understand what a sign means, but at least understands that it is a sign, is not in fact subjected to slavery. It is better to be dominated by unknown but useful signs than to interpret them in a useless way and so thrust one's neck, rescued from the yoke of slavery, into the toils of error.

As well as this rule, which warns us not to pursue a figurative 33 (that is, metaphorical) expression as if it were literal, we must add a further one: not to accept a literal one as if it were figurative. We must first explain the way to discover whether an expression is literal or figurative. Generally speaking, it is this: anything in the divine discourse that cannot be related either to good morals or to the true faith should be taken as figurative. Good morals have to do with our love of God and our neigh- 34 bour, the true faith with our understanding of God and our

neighbour. The hope that each person has within his own conscience is directly related to the progress that he feels himself
to be making towards the love and understanding of God and
his neighbour. All this has been dealt with in Book 1.

35   But since the human race is prone to judge sins not by the
strength of the actual lust, but rather by the standard of its own
practices, people generally regard as culpable only such actions
as men of their own time and place tend to blame and condemn, and regard as commendable and praiseworthy only
such actions as are acceptable within the conventions of their
own society. And so it happens that if scripture enjoins something at variance with the practices of its readers, or censures
something that is not at variance with them, they consider the
relevant expression to be figurative (always assuming that their

36   minds are governed by the authority of the Word). But scripture enjoins nothing but love, and censures nothing but lust,
and moulds men's minds accordingly. Similarly, if their minds
are taken over by a particular prejudice, people consider as figurative anything that scripture asserts to the contrary. But it
asserts nothing except the catholic faith, in time past, present,
and future. It narrates the past, foretells the future, and
demonstrates the present, but all these things serve to nourish
and strengthen this love, and to overcome and annihilate lust.

37   By love I mean the impulse of one's mind to enjoy God on his
own account and to enjoy oneself and one's neighbour on
account of God;* and by lust I mean the impulse of one's mind
to enjoy oneself and one's neighbour and any corporeal thing
not on account of God. What unbridled lust does to corrupt a
person's own mind and body is called wickedness; what it does

38   to harm another person is called wrongdoing. All sins can be
divided into these two kinds, but wickedness comes first. Once
it has depleted the mind and as it were bankrupted it, it rushes
on to commit wrongdoing in order to remove the obstacles to
wickedness or to find assistance for it. Similarly, what love
does to benefit itself is self-interest, and what it does to benefit
a neighbour is known as kindness. And here self-interest
comes first, because nobody can do good to another out of
resources which he does not possess. The more the realm of
lust is destroyed, the more the realm of love is increased.

Any harsh and even cruel word or deed attributed to God or 39
his saints that is found in the holy scriptures applies to the
destruction of the realm of lust. If the message is clear, it
should not be treated as figurative and related to something
else. For example, Paul's saying [Rom. 2: 5–9]: 'You are stor-
ing up wrath for yourself on the day of wrath, the day of the
revelation of the just judgement of God, who will repay all people according to their works; eternal life to those who by persistence in well-doing seek glory and honour and immortality,
but anger and fury to those who fractiously refuse to obey the
truth and put their trust in iniquity. There will be tribulation
and distress to every soul of man that does evil, first to the Jew
and then to the Greek.' But this was written to those whose 40
destruction must accompany that of the lust itself, those who
refused to overcome it. In cases where the realm of lust is overcome by a person once dominated by it, this perfectly clear saying applies: 'Those who belong to Jesus Christ have crucified
their flesh along with its passions and desires' [Gal. 5: 24].
Even here, admittedly, some words are used metaphorically,
such as 'wrath of God' and 'crucified', but they are not so 41
many, or so unclear in expression, as to hide the sense and create allegory or obscurity, which is what I mean by figurative
expression in the strict sense. On the other hand, Jeremiah's
phrase, 'Behold today I have established you over nations and
kingdoms, to uproot and destroy, to lay waste and scatter' [Jer.
1: 10], is, without doubt, entirely figurative, and so must be
related to the aim that I mentioned above.

Matters which seem like wickedness to the unenlightened, 42
whether merely spoken or actually performed, whether attributed to God or to people whose holiness is commended to us,
are entirely figurative. Such mysteries are to be elucidated in
terms of the need to nourish love. A person who makes more
limited use of transient things than the moral conventions of
his own society allow is either self-controlled or superstitious;
a person whose use of them exceeds the limits set by the practice of good people in his society is either guilty of wickedness
or an indication of some special significance. In all such matters 43
what is reprehensible is not the use made of things but the
user's desire. No person in his right mind should ever think

that the Lord's feet were anointed by a woman with precious
ointment [Matt. 26: 7–12; John 12: 1–7] in the same way as the
feet of self-indulgent and evil men are anointed at the sort of
banquets which we abhor. A good perfume signifies a good
reputation: anyone who enjoys this through the deeds of an
upright life anoints Christ's feet in a figurative sense with a
44 most precious perfume by following in his footsteps. Again,
what is generally speaking wicked in other people is the sign of
something great in one who is divine or a prophet. Consorting
with a prostitute is one thing in a depraved society, but something quite different in the prophecy of Hosea [Hos. 1: 2–3].
And the fact that some people strip in their drunken, uninhib-
ited parties does not make it immoral to be naked in the bath.

45   We must therefore pay careful attention to the conduct
appropriate to different places, times, and persons, in case we
make rash imputations of wickedness. It is possible for a wise
man to take some kind of costly food without any taint of greed
or gluttony, and for an unwise one to yearn for junk food with
a most disgusting outburst of greed. Or someone might have a
healthy preference for eating fish, like our Lord [Luke 24: 42],
rather than lentils, like Abraham's grandson Esau [Gen.
46 25: 34], or barley, like cattle. The fact that most animals are
more restrained than we are is not the result of their cheaper
diet. In all matters of this kind actions are made acceptable or
unacceptable not by the particular things we make use of, but
by our motives for using them and our methods of seeking
47 them. Righteous men of long ago visualized the kingdom of
heaven as an earthly kingdom, and predicted it accordingly. In
the interests of perpetuating the race there was a perfectly
blameless practice for one man to have several wives. For the
same reason it was not honourable for one woman to have several
husbands; that does not make a woman more fertile, and it is
indeed a form of immoral prostitution to seek either profit or
48 progeny through promiscuity. Given such social conventions,
things that the saints of those ages could do without any lust—
although they were doing something which cannot be done
without lust nowadays—are not censured by scripture. Anything of this kind related there is to be understood not only his-
torically and literally but also figuratively and prophetically,

and interpreted according to the aim of love, whether it be love of God or love of one's neighbour, or both. In ancient Rome it 49 was considered wicked to wear ankle-length tunics or ones with sleeves,* whereas now it is thought immoral for the upper classes not to have them when wearing tunics; so we must observe that in the use of all other such things there must be an absence of lust, which not only wickedly exploits the actual practice of its society but also, by going beyond those limits in an outburst of total wickedness, often makes a disgraceful exhibition of its own ugliness, which had previously been concealed behind the barriers of traditional morality.

Whatever accords with the social practices of those with 50 whom we have to live this present life—whether this manner of life is imposed by necessity or undertaken in the course of duty—should be related by good and serious men to the aims of self-interest and kindness, either literally, as we ourselves should do, or also figuratively, as is allowed to the prophets. When those who are unfamiliar with different social practices 51 come up against such actions in their reading, they think them wicked unless restrained by some explicit authority. They are incapable of realizing that their own sort of behaviour patterns, whether in matters of marriage, or diet, or dress, or any other aspect of human life and culture, would seem wicked to other races or other ages. Some people have been struck by the enor- 52 mous diversity of social practices and in a state of drowsiness, as I would put it—for they were neither sunk in the deep sleep of stupidity nor capable of staying awake to greet the light of wisdom—have concluded that justice has no absolute existence but that each race views its own practices as just.* So since the practices of all races are diverse, whereas justice ought to remain unchangeable, there clearly is no such thing as justice anywhere. To say no more, they have not realized that the injunction 'do not do to another what you would not wish to be done to yourself' [Tobit 4: 16] can in no way be modified by racial differences. When this injunction is related to the love of 53 God, all wickedness dies; and when it is related to the love of one's neighbour, all wrongdoing dies. For nobody wants his own dwelling to be wrecked, and so he should not wish to wreck God's dwelling (which is himself). Nobody wants to be

harmed by anybody; so he should not do harm to anybody.
54 So when the tyranny of lust has been overthrown love rules
with laws that are utterly just: to love God on his account, and
to love oneself and one's neighbour on God's account. Therefore in dealing with figurative expressions we will observe a
rule of this kind: the passage being read should be studied with
careful consideration until its interpretation can be connected
with the realm of love. If this point is made literally, then no
kind of figurative expression need be considered.

55   If the expression is a prescriptive one, and either forbids
wickedness or wrongdoing, or enjoins self-interest or kindness, it is not figurative. But if it appears to enjoin wickedness
or wrongdoing or to forbid self-interest or kindness, it is figurative. Scripture says, 'Unless you eat the flesh of the Son of
Man and drink his blood, you will not have life in you' [John
6: 54]. This appears to enjoin wickedness or wrongdoing, and
so it is figurative, a command to participate in the Lord's
passion and to store in our memory the pleasurable and useful
knowledge that his flesh was crucified and wounded for our
56 sake. Scripture says, 'If your enemy is hungry, feed him; if he
is thirsty, give him a drink' [Rom. 12: 20]. Here no one can
doubt that it enjoins kindness. But one would think that the
following words, 'for by doing this you will pile coals of fire on
his head', advocate malicious wrongdoing; so one can be sure
that it was meant figuratively. Given that it can be interpreted
in two ways, in the sense of causing harm and in the sense of
offering something, the principle of love should lead you to the
interpretation involving kindness, so that you understand by
'coals of fire' the agonized groans of penitence which cure the
pride of a person who regrets having been the enemy of some-
57 one who helped him in distress. Similarly, when the Lord says,
'He who loves his own soul shall lose it'* [John 12: 25], this
should not be taken as forbidding self-interest (everyone must
seek to preserve his own soul) but as meaning 'lose one's soul'
in a figurative sense—that is, to destroy and lose one's current
perverse and disordered way of using it, by which one is
inclined to what is temporal and prevented from seeking what
is eternal. It is written: 'give to the merciful and do not support
a sinner' [Ecclus. 12: 4]. The second part of this statement

seems to forbid kindness ('do not support a sinner'); so understand 'sinner' figuratively as 'sin', the meaning being 'do not
support his sin'.

It often happens that someone who is, or thinks he is, at a 58
higher stage of the spiritual life regards as figurative instructions which are given to those at a lower stage. So, for example,
a man who has embraced a life of celibacy and castrated himself
for the sake of the kingdom of heaven [Matt. 19: 12] might
maintain that any instructions given in the sacred books about
loving or governing one's wife should be taken not literally but
figuratively; or someone who has resolved to keep his own
daughter unmarried might try to interpret as figurative the
saying 'Marry off your daughter, and you will have done a
great deed' [Ecclus. 7: 27]. This too, then, will be one of our 59
rules for interpreting scripture: we must understand that some
instructions are given to all people alike, but others to particular classes of people, so that the medicine may confront not
only the general pathology of the disease but also the particular
weakness of each part of the body. What cannot be raised to a
higher level must be healed at its own level.

Likewise we must take care not to regard something in the 60
Old Testament that is by the standards of its own time not
wickedness or wrongdoing, even when understood literally
and not figuratively, as capable of being transferred to the
present time and applied to our own lives. A person will not do
this unless lust is in total control and actively seeking the com-
plicity of the very scriptures by which it must be overthrown.
Such a wretch does not realize that these things are written
down for a useful purpose, to enable men of good conscience
to see, for their own spiritual health, that a practice which
they reject can have a good application, and that a practice
which they embrace can be damnable, if the love shown by its
followers (in the first case) or their greed (in the second) is
taken into account.

For if one man according to the custom of his time could be 61
chaste with many wives, another today can be lustful with a
single wife. I approve the man who exploits the fertility of
many women for a purpose other than sexual gratification
more highly than one who enjoys one woman's flesh for its own

sake. In one case there is the motive of self-interest, in accordance with the conditions prevailing at the time; in the other, the satisfaction of a lust caught up in the pleasures of the world. In God's eyes the men to whom the apostle allowed sexual intercourse with their individual wives, because of their lack of self-control [1 Cor. 7: 2], are at a lower stage than those who each had several wives but looked only to the procreation of children in the sexual act (just as in eating and drinking a wise

62 man looks only to physical health). And so if the Lord's advent had found them still in this life, when it was time not 'to throw away stones but collect them' [Eccles. 3: 5], they would have immediately castrated themselves for the sake of the kingdom of heaven. For there is no difficulty in forgoing sex, except where there is lust in practising it. Those men of old knew that the enjoyment of sex with their wives was a form of unrestrained abuse. This is shown by Tobit's prayer when he married his wife: 'You are blessed, Lord of our fathers, and your name is blessed for ages to come. Let the heavens and all creation bless you. You made Adam and gave him the assistance of Eve. And now, Lord, you know that it is not for enjoyment that I am taking my sister, but in all honesty, so that you may have

63 mercy on us, O Lord' [Tobit 8: 7–10]. But promiscuous people who with unbridled lust go through one affair after another, or people who, just with a single wife, not only exceed the limit appropriate to the procreation of children but also in their inhuman incontinence pile filth upon filth with an utterly shameless exercise of their slavish kind of freedom, do not consider it possible that the men of old treated their many wives with self-control and in so doing simply fulfilled the duty, required by their times, of continuing the race. What they themselves, entangled as they are in the toils of lust, do not even achieve with one wife, they think totally impossible with several.

64   But they may as well say that good and holy men should not even be honoured or praised, just because they themselves, when honoured and praised, swell with pride, and because the more frequent, and the more widespread, the publicity of flattering tongues becomes, the more greedy they are for empty praise. This makes them vain, and so the wind of rumour,

whether it is seen as favourable or unfavourable, draws them
into various whirlpools of wickedness or drives them against
the rocks of wrongdoing. So they should realize what a difficult
and demanding thing it is not to be enticed by the bait of praise
or pierced by the barbs of insult, and not measure others by
themselves. They would do better to reckon that our apostles 65
were neither puffed up when admired by men nor cast down
when despised. They escaped neither of these temptations,
being fêted by the accolades of believers and slandered by the
abuse of persecutors. So just as the apostles experienced all this 66
in accordance with the custom of their times without being
corrupted, so those men of old, relating their treatment of
women to the conventions of their times, did not tolerate the
domination of lust, the lust which enslaves men who find all
this incredible.

And so if they discovered that their wives or concubines had 67
been accosted or violated by their sons, these men would be
quite unable to restrain themselves from implacably hating
them, supposing that something of this kind had happened to
them. But King David, when he suffered this at the hands of 68
his wicked and brutal son, not only put up with his cruelty but
even lamented his death [2 Kgs. (2 Sam.) 18: 33]. He was not
trapped in the net of carnal jealousy, since it was not his own
injuries but the sins of his son that worried him. He had in fact
deliberately given orders that if his son were overcome he
should not be killed, so as to leave him some scope for repentance when overthrown [2 Kgs. (2 Sam.) 18: 5]. After failing to
save him he grieved over his son's death not because of his
bereavement, but because he knew the penalties to which a
soul guilty of such wicked adultery and murder was heading.
For on the death of his earlier son (who was innocent), whose
illness had been distressing him [2 Kgs. (2 Sam.) 12: 15–23], he
was pleased. The following episode makes it very clear what 69
moderation and self-control those men showed towards
women. The same king, his head turned by youthful passion
and worldly success, unlawfully violated a woman after ordering her husband to be killed [2 Kgs. (2 Sam.) 11], and was
accused by a prophet [2 Kgs. (2 Sam.) 12: 1–14]. When he
came to David to convict him of his sin, Nathan put to him the

analogy of a poor man with one sheep, and a neighbour of the poor man, who, although he himself had several, nevertheless served his poor neighbour's one and only sheep to greet the
70 arrival of a guest. This appalled King David, who ordered the neighbour to be killed and the poor man to be compensated for his sheep four times over—and so condemned himself unawares for the sin he was aware of having committed. When apprised of this and warned of divine punishment he atoned for his sin by repentance. But in this analogy it is only the sexual sin that is signalled by the sheep of the poor neighbour. David was not asked in this analogy about the murder of the woman's husband—the killing of the poor man himself, that is, with his single sheep—and so it was on his adultery alone
71 that he issued his self-condemnatory verdict. From this one can infer the self-control with which he treated his many women, since in the case of the one woman with whom he had overstepped the limit he was compelled to punish himself. But in David's case there was no permanence to this extravagant lust, it was a passing phase; that is why his illicit appetite was called a 'guest' by the prophet who convicted him. He did not say that the man had offered his poor neighbour's sheep in a
72 feast for his king, but for his guest. But in David's son Solomon this lust was no guest paying a passing visit, but took over the whole kingdom. Scripture did not remain silent about this, but condemned him as a womanizer [3 Kgs. (1 Kgs.) 11: 1–4]. In his early life he had a passionate desire for wisdom; but then, after gaining it through spiritual love, he lost it through carnal love.

73   So all, or nearly all, of the deeds contained in the books of the Old Testament are to be interpreted not only literally but also figuratively; but (in the case of those which the reader interprets literally) if agents are praised but their actions do not agree with the practices of the good men who since the Lord's coming in the flesh have been the guardians of the divine precepts, one should take up the figurative meaning into the understanding* but not take over the deed itself into one's own behaviour. Many things were done in those times out of duty
74 which cannot be done now except out of lust. But when reading about the sins of great men, even if it is possible to observe or trace a prefiguration of future events in them, one should

nevertheless take on board the literal meaning of the act, in this way. Bearing in mind the dangerous storms and miserable shipwrecks suffered by great men one should refrain from boasting of one's own deeds, which would be quite wrong, or despising others as sinners by the standards of one's own justice. Even the sins of these men have been recorded in order to put people everywhere in awe of the apostle's saying, 'So whoever thinks he stands must take care not to fall' [1 Cor. 10: 12]. There is hardly a page in the Bible which does not proclaim the message: 'God resists the proud, but gives grace to the humble' [Jas. 4: 6]. 75

The greatest care must therefore be taken to determine whether the expression that we are trying to understand is literal or figurative. When we have worked out that it is figurative, it is easy to study it from various angles, using the rules set out in Book 1, until we reach the true meaning, especially if we have the advantage of experience fortified by the exercise of holiness. We find out if an expression is literal or figurative by considering the criteria mentioned above. Once this becomes clear, the words in which it is expressed will be found to be taken either from things that are similar or things that are in some way connected. But since there are many ways in which things may resemble other things, we should not imagine that there is a hard and fast rule that a word will always have the meaning that it has in a particular place. The Lord used the word 'leaven' in a pejorative sense when he said 'Beware of the leaven of the Pharisees' [Matt. 16: 6, 11], but in a commendatory sense when he said, 'The kingdom of heaven is like a woman who hid leaven in three measures of wheat until it was all leavened' [Luke 13: 21].* 76 77 78

Examination of these differences reveals two forms. The various meanings of a particular thing may be either contrary or just different. By contrary I mean cases in which a particular thing is used sometimes in a good sense and sometimes in a bad one, like the leaven just discussed. Another example is 'lion', which signifies Christ in the passage 'The lion from the tribe of Judah has conquered' [Rev. 5: 5], but 'devil' in the passage 'Your enemy the devil walks round like a roaring lion, seeking someone to devour' [1 Pet. 5: 8]. And 'serpent' is used 79 80 in a good sense in the passage 'be wise as serpents' [Matt. 10: 16], but in a bad sense in 'the serpent seduced Eve by its cunning' [2 Cor. 11: 3]. 'Bread' in a good sense: 'I am the living bread come from heaven' [John 6: 51]; in a bad sense: 'gladly eat hidden bread' [Prov. 9: 17]. And so on. The examples cited are quite uncontroversial in meaning, since only perfectly plain passages should be cited as examples. But there are some which are uncertain, such as 'There is a cup of wine in the hand 81 of the Lord, full of mixed wine' [Ps. 74: 9 (75: 8)]. It is not clear whether this signifies the wrath of God, not carried as far as the ultimate penalty (that is, down to the dregs), or the gracious gift of the scriptures which passes from Jews to Gentiles (because 'it inclined from the one to the other'), but in such a way that the practices redolent of the flesh remain with the Jews ('because its dregs are not emptied'). A thing may be used not with a contrary significance, but just with a different one; an example is 'water', which signifies both people, as in Revelation [Rev. 17: 15], and the Holy Spirit, as in 'rivers of running water will flow from his belly' [John 7: 38], as well as various other things, depending on the context.

82   There are other things too which signify not just single ideas but, taken individually, two or often more ideas, depending on 83 the contexts in which they are found. From passages where such things are expressed clearly one should find out how they are to be understood in obscure contexts. There is no better way of understanding what was said to the Lord in the words 'Take your arms and shield and rise to help me' [Ps. 34: 2 (35: 2)] than by using the passage 'Lord, you have crowned us as with the shield of your goodwill' [Ps. 5: 13 (5: 12)]. Not that we should understand only the meaning 'God's goodwill' in every passage where we read of the shield being used as a defence; there is also 'the shield of faith, with which you may extinguish all the arrows of the evil one' [Eph. 6: 16]. Nor again should we necessarily assign the meaning 'faith' to the shield alone among such spiritual armour; in another passage the breastplate of faith is also mentioned: 'Put on the breastplate of faith and love' [1 Thess. 5: 8].

84   Sometimes not just one meaning but two or more meanings are perceived in the same words of scripture. Even if the

writer's meaning is obscure, there is no danger here, provided
that it can be shown from other passages of the holy scriptures
that each of these interpretations is consistent with the truth.
The person examining the divine utterances must of course do
his best to arrive at the intention of the writer through whom
the Holy Spirit produced that part of scripture; he may reach
that meaning or carve out from the words another meaning
which does not run counter to the faith, using the evidence of
any other passage of the divine utterances. Perhaps the author   85
too saw that very meaning in the words which we are trying to
understand. Certainly the spirit of God who worked through
the author foresaw without any doubt that it would present
itself to a reader or listener, or rather planned that it should
present itself, because it too is based on the truth. Could God
have built into the divine eloquence a more generous or boun-
tiful gift than the possibility of understanding the same words
in several ways, all of them deriving confirmation from other
no less divinely inspired passages?* When one unearths an   86
equivocal meaning which cannot be verified by unequivocal
support from the holy scriptures it remains for the meaning to
be brought into the open by a process of reasoning, even if the
writer whose words we are seeking to understand perhaps did
not perceive it. But this practice is dangerous; it is much safer
to operate within the divine scriptures. When we wish to
examine passages made obscure by metaphorical expressions,
the result should be something which is beyond dispute or
which, if not beyond dispute, can be settled by finding and
deploying corroboratory evidence from within scripture itself.

The literary-minded should be aware that our Christian   87
authors used all the figures of speech which teachers of
grammar call by their Greek name of tropes, and that they
did so more diversely and profusely than can be judged or
imagined by those who are unfamiliar with scripture or who
gained their knowledge of figures from other literature.*
Those who know about these tropes recognize them in sacred
literature, and this knowledge to some extent helps them
in understanding it. This would not be the proper place to
present them to people not familiar with them; I do not wish to
look as if I am giving a course on grammar. I recommend that

they be learnt independently; as indeed I have recommended
already, in Book 2, when discussing the importance of learning
88 languages.* (Letters, from which grammar actually takes its
name—the Greek word for them is *grammata*—are of course
the signs of the sounds involved in the articulation of the words
which we use when speaking.) In the divine books we find
not only examples of these tropes, as of everything else, but
also the names of some of them, like 'allegory', 'enigma', and
'parable'.* Almost all these tropes, which are said to be
acquired through one of the 'liberal' arts,* are also found in the
utterances of those who have had no formal teaching in gram-
89 mar and are content with the style of ordinary people. Don't
we all say 'so may you flourish'? This is a metaphor. Don't we
all refer to a swimming pool by the word *piscina*, which takes its
name from fish even though it does not contain fish and was not
made for fish?* This trope is called catachresis.*
90   It would take a long time to work through the others in the
same way. Popular speech has even come to use some which
are remarkable because what they mean is the opposite of what
is said, like the figures of irony and antiphrasis. In irony we indi-
cate what is meant by means of our intonation, as when we say to
a man who is doing something badly, 'you're doing a good job
there'. In antiphrasis, on the other hand, we signify the opposite
meaning, not by our intonation, but either by the use of particular words whose origin derives from a contrary—for example,
lucus [grove], which is so called because it has little light,* or by
using certain customary expressions (though these can also be
used without a contrary meaning). For example, when looking
for something that is not available in a particular place, we may
be told 'there's plenty';* or we may by adding words give what
we say a contrary interpretation, as in 'beware of him, he's a good
91 man'.* Are things of this kind not said by all the uneducated*
and by people who are totally ignorant of the tropes and all their
names? A knowledge of them is necessary for the resolution of
ambiguities in scripture because when a meaning based on the
literal interpretation of the words is absurd we must investigate
whether the passage that we cannot understand is perhaps being
expressed by means of one or other of the tropes. This is how
most hidden meanings have been discovered.

A certain Tyconius,* who although a Donatist himself 92
wrote against the Donatists with irresistible power—and
thereby stands convicted of having a split personality since he
was unwilling to make a clean break with them—wrote a book
which he called *The Book of Rules*,* because in it he developed
seven rules which could be used like keys to open up the secrets
of the divine scriptures. The first rule is 'On the Lord and his 93
body'; the second 'On the Lord's twofold body'; the third 'On
the promises and the law'; the fourth 'On species and genus';
the fifth 'On measurements of time'; the sixth 'On recapitulation'; the seventh 'On the devil and his body'. Consideration of
these rules, as expounded by him, is quite helpful in penetrating the obscure parts of the divine writings. Of course not
everything that is written in a way that makes it difficult to
understand can be clarified by these rules; there are numerous
other methods not included in his seven, and indeed Tyconius
himself explains many problems without applying any of these
rules, because they are not needed. Sometimes there is no 94
relevant matter or problem in the passage under investigation;
as, for example, when in Revelation* he discusses how to
interpret the angels of the seven churches to which John was
ordered to write [Rev. 1: 20]. There he argues in many different ways and reaches the conclusion that we should interpret
the angels as the churches. In that very full discussion there is
no sign of these rules, and yet the problem is certainly a
very abstruse one. But enough of examples: it would take too
much time and effort to assemble all the abstruse passages in
scripture where recourse to these seven rules is unnecessary.

When Tyconius was presenting these so-called rules he 95
claimed for them the power to make intelligible almost all the
abstruse passages that we find in the law (meaning the divine
books), if they are properly learnt and applied. He began his
book by saying, 'I have thought it particularly necessary, and
more pressing than anything else, to write a book of rules and
as it were to fashion some keys, or spotlights, to reveal
the secrets of the law. There are certain mystical rules which
govern the secret passages of the entire law and make the
treasures of the truth invisible to some people. If the principle
of these rules is accepted in the ungrudging spirit with which

I offer them, all closed doors will swing open and all obscurity
be as light as day, so that the reader who roams through the vast
forest of prophecy will be guided by these rules as by so many
96 illuminated pathways, and be preserved from error.'* Had he
said here, 'there are certain mystical rules which govern some
secret passages of the law', or even 'which govern some important secret passages of the law', and not 'the secret passages of
the whole law', and had he not said, 'all closed doors will swing
open' but 'many closed doors will swing open', he would have
been telling the truth without raising false hopes in his readers
and disciples by attributing to his careful and useful work more
than the facts warranted. I thought that this needed saying so
97 that students would actually read the book itself—it is very
helpful for understanding the scriptures—but not expect from
it more than it has to offer. It must certainly be read with
caution, not only because of certain things which, being
human, he gets wrong, but especially because of the things
which he says as a Donatist heretic. I will now briefly explain
the teaching and advice that these seven rules have to offer.*

98   The first one is 'On the Lord and his body'. Sometimes we
know that a single being, consisting of a head and a body, that
is, Christ and his church, is being presented to us; for it was
said to the faithful, not without reason, 'so you are the seed of
Abraham' [Gal. 3: 29], although there is but a single seed of
Abraham, namely Christ. In such cases we should not be
puzzled when scripture moves from head to body or vice versa,
99 while still dealing with one and the same person. For it is a
single person that says, 'He has placed a garland on me as on a
husband and has arrayed me with ornament like a wife' [Isa.
61: 10], but it is of course necessary to appreciate which of
these two statements applies to the head (Christ), and which to
the body (the church).

100   The second rule is 'On the Lord's twofold body', but he
should not have given it this title, since something that will not
be with God for ever is not in fact the Lord's body. He should
rather have said 'On the Lord's true and mixed body', or 'true
and apparent body', or perhaps something else, because false
Christians should not be said to be with God even at the
present time, let alone for eternity, although they appear to be

within his church. So that rule could also have been entitled 'On the mixed church'. This rule demands close concentration 101 from the student, since scripture, though actually speaking to another set of people, may seem to be speaking to the actual persons it was addressing before, or may seem to be speaking about the same persons when in fact it is speaking about others, as if both kinds formed a single body by virtue of their temporary unity and their participation in the sacraments. A sentence in the Song of Songs is relevant here: 'I am dark and pretty like the tents of Kedar, like the curtains of Solomon' [S. of S. 1: 4]. She does not say, 'I was dark like the tents of Kedar and I am pretty like the curtains of Solomon', but instead says that she is both, because of the temporal unity of good and bad fish inside the single net [cf. Matt. 13: 47–8]. The tents of Kedar refer to Ishmael, who will not be the heir with the free woman's son [Gen. 21: 10; Gal. 4: 30]. And so although 102 God says about the good part, 'I shall lead the blind along a way unknown to them, and they will tread paths unknown to them; and I shall make darkness into light for them and crooked ways into straight ones. I shall perform what I say and will not desert them', he says shortly afterwards of the other part, the bad part mixed in with them, 'but they themselves have turned back', although other people are meant by these words [Isa. 42: 16–17]. Because they are now together, he seems to be speaking of those about whom he was speaking before; but they will not always be together. In fact they are like the slave mentioned in the gospel, whose master will when he arrives set him apart and place his lot with the false Christians [Matt. 24: 50–1].

The third rule is 'On the promises and the law', though an 103 alternative title might be 'On the spirit and the letter', as I myself called it when writing on this subject.* It could also be called 'On grace and commandment'. But this seems to me an important problem in itself, rather than a rule to be applied to solving problems. This is the issue that the Pelagians failed to understand when creating, or developing, their heresy. In his discussion of this Tyconius worked on it effectively, but not exhaustively. For when discussing faith and works he said that 104 works were given to us by God according to the merit of our faith, but that faith itself came from within us without coming

to us from God. He did not take note of the apostle's words:
'peace to the brethren and love with faith from God the Father
and the Lord Jesus Christ' [Eph. 6: 23]. Tyconius had no experience of the heresy which sprang up in our time and was a great
trial to me as I championed the grace of God which comes
through the Lord Jesus Christ; a heresy which, in accordance
with the apostle's words, 'it is right that there be heresies, so
that the genuine among you may be recognized' [1 Cor. 11: 19],
made me more alert and careful, with the result that I noticed
in the holy scripture something that had escaped Tyconius,
who was less attentive and less on his guard because he had no
opponent: namely that even faith itself is a gift of God, who
distributes to each individual his or her measure [Rom. 12: 3].

105 In accordance with this truth it was said to certain people, 'a
privilege has been given to you for the sake of Christ: that you
should not only believe in him, but also suffer for him' [Phil.
1: 29]. Who can doubt that both things are the gift of God, on
hearing—with faith and understanding—that both have been
given? There are many other testimonies that demonstrate
this, but that is not my present purpose. I have, however, dealt
with them very often in various other places.

106   The fourth of Tyconius' rules is 'On species and genus'.
That is his title; by 'species' he means a part, by 'genus' the
whole to which the part which he calls the species belongs. So
since each individual state is part of the whole of the world's
population, he calls this the species, and the whole population
the genus. We need not here apply the subtle distinctions
taught by the logicians, who argue very finely about the
107 difference between part and species. The same principle
applies to anything of this nature found in the divine writings
which concerns not a single state, but a single province or
nation or kingdom. For example: not only are statements made
in the holy scriptures about Jerusalem or about Gentile states
such as Tyre, Babylon, or whatever, which transcend the
limits of the particular state and are more suitable to all races,
but statements are also made about Judaea, Egypt, Assyria, and
other nations in which there are several states but which do
not amount to the whole world but only a part of it, and these
statements transcend the limits of the particular nation and are

more suitable to the whole world of which that is a part or, in his terms, to the genus of which it is a species. In this sense these words have entered the popular domain: even laymen can understand what is of general or specific import in an imperial edict. The rule applies to persons, too: witness the things said about Solomon, which transcend the limits of their subject and in fact really become clear only when related to Christ or the church, of which Solomon is a part. 108

The species is not always transcended: often statements are made which are quite clearly appropriate either to the species as well as the genus or perhaps exclusively to the species. But when scripture moves from species to genus while apparently still speaking of the species, the reader's attention must be particularly close, so as not to seek in the species a meaning which can be found more easily and convincingly in the genus. It is easy to understand what the prophet Ezekiel says: 'The house of Israel lived in the land and they profaned it by their ways and their idols and their sins; their conduct before my face was like the uncleanness of a menstruating woman. And I poured out my anger upon them and dispersed them among the peoples and scattered them among all regions; I judged them according to their ways and according to their sins' [Ezek. 36: 17–19]. It is easy, I say, to understand this of the house of Israel, about which Paul says 'see Israel according to the flesh' [1 Cor. 10: 18], because the people of Israel did or experienced all these things in the flesh. Other things in what follows can also be understood of that people. But when he goes on to say, 'And I will sanctify my name, that great name which is profaned among the nations, which you profaned in the midst of them; and the nations will know that I am the Lord' [Ezek. 36: 23], the reader must now carefully observe how the species is transcended and the genus introduced. The passage continues: 'When I am sanctified through you before their eyes, I will take you from the peoples and gather you from all lands and bring you into your own land. And I will sprinkle you with clean water, and you will be made clean from all your idolatries. I will cleanse you and give you a new heart, and I will give you a new spirit. And I will take away from your flesh the heart of stone and give you a heart of flesh; and I will give my 109 110 111

spirit to you and cause you to walk in my ordinances and keep and observe my judgements. And you will live in the land which I gave to your fathers, and you will be my people and I will be your God. And I will cleanse you from all your
112 uncleanliness' [Ezek. 36: 23–9]. That this is a prophecy about the New Testament, involving not only that particular race in its remnants (about which it is written elsewhere, 'Even if the number of the sons of Israel is as the sand of the seashore, only a remnant will be safe') [Isa. 10: 22; cf. Rom. 9: 27] but also all the other races promised to their fathers, who are also our fathers, will be unambiguously clear to anyone who has the insight to see that here is a promise of the baptism of regeneration [Titus 3: 5], which we now see duly given to all peoples. He will also realize and recognize that the words used by Paul the apostle to commend the grace of the New Testament so that it stood out in comparison with the Old Testament—'You are our letter, written not with ink but with the spirit of the living God, not on tablets of stone but on the fleshly tablets of the heart' [2 Cor. 3: 2–3]—derive from this passage, where the prophet says, 'And I will give you a new heart and a new spirit, and I will take away from your flesh the heart of stone and give
113 you a heart of flesh' [Ezek. 36: 26]. He wanted the heart of flesh—whence the apostle's expression 'on the fleshly tablets of the heart'—to be distinguished from the heart of stone because of its sentient life; and by sentient life he meant intelligent life. So 'spiritual Israel' becomes not a matter of a single race, but of all the races promised to the fathers in their seed, which is Christ [Gal. 3: 16].
114 This spiritual Israel is distinguished from the fleshly Israel, consisting of a single people, by the novelty of grace, not by nobility of race, and by mentality, not nationality. But such is the prophet's profundity that while speaking about the former and indeed to the former he moves imperceptibly to the latter; and while speaking about the latter or addressing himself to the latter he still seems to be speaking about the former and addressing himself to the former, not with the hostile purpose of begrudging us an understanding of the scriptures but with
115 the healthy one of stretching our understanding. So when he says 'I will bring you into your own land' [Ezek. 36: 24], and a

little later repeats it, 'And you will live in the land which I gave to your fathers' [Ezek. 36: 28], we should understand this not carnally, of the fleshly Israel, but spiritually, of the spiritual Israel. It is the church 'without blemish or wrinkle' [Eph. 5: 27], assembled from all peoples and destined to reign with Christ, which is itself the land of the blessed, 'the land of the living' [Ps. 26: 13 (27: 13)]. And it is the church itself that should be understood as having been given to the fathers at the time when it was promised by God's sure and immutable will, since what our fathers believed would be given in its own time was already given with the security of promise or predestination. Similarly, when writing to Timothy of the grace given to the saints, Paul says, 'Not according to our works, but according to his purpose and his grace, which was given to us in Christ Jesus before the eternal ages but has now been made plain by our saviour's coming' [2 Tim. 1: 9–10]. He said that 116 grace was given at a time when there were not even people to whom it could be given, because in God's disposition and foreknowledge what was going to happen in its own time had already happened; this he describes by the words 'made plain'. However, this could also be understood to mean the land of a future generation, since there will be 'a new heaven and a new earth' [Rev. 21: 1], in which the unjust will not be able to live. Therefore it is said to the saints quite correctly that the land itself, which will not in any way belong to the wicked, is theirs; because, in the same way, the land was actually given at the time when the gift was ratified.

The fifth rule laid down by Tyconius is the one that he calls 117 'On measurements of time', by which one can often discover or figure out indications of time in the holy scriptures that are not explicit. He says that this rule works in two ways, either through the trope of synecdoche or through ordinary numbers. The trope of synecdoche permits either the whole to be understood from the part, or the part from the whole. By way of example, one evangelist says that an event happened eight days later and another puts it six days later—this being the occasion when on the mountain with only three disciples present the Lord's face shone like the sun and his clothes like snow.* These statements about the number of days could not 118 both be correct unless the writer who said 'eight days later' is understood as having treated the last part of the day on which Christ predicted that the event would happen and the first part of the day on which he demonstrated its fulfilment as two whole days, and the writer who said 'after six days' as having counted six whole days, but only the intervening ones. This figure of speech, by which the whole is signified by a part, also provides a solution to the problem about Christ's resurrection.

119 For unless the last part of the day on which he suffered is taken as one whole day (by adding the previous night) and the night at the end of which he rose again as another whole day (by adding the Sunday that was just dawning), you cannot get the three days and nights which he predicted that he would spend

120 in the heart of the earth [Matt. 12: 40]. By ordinary numbers he means those which scripture makes conspicuous use of, like the numbers seven or ten or twelve, and the others which scholars happily acknowledge as they read. As a rule such numbers are made to stand for a complete period of time; so 'I will praise you seven times a day' [Ps. 118: 164 (119: 164)] means exactly the same as 'his praise shall always be on my lips'

121 [Ps. 33: 2 (34: 1)]. They have the same meaning when multiplied, whether by ten, giving seventy or seven hundred— hence the seventy years of Jeremiah [Jer. 25: 11, 29: 10] may be understood spiritually as the whole of the time during which the church is among foreigners—or by themselves; so ten times ten is a hundred, and twelve times twelve is one hundred and forty-four, a number which in Revelation signifies the whole body of saints [Rev. 7: 4]. So it is clear not only that these numbers are the key to chronological problems, but also that their significance is wider and their influence far-reaching. For in Revelation the number I mentioned relates not to time, but people.

122 Tyconius gives the name 'Recapitulation' to his sixth rule, a rule discovered by close attention to the obscurities of scripture. Some passages are presented as if their contents follow in chronological order or in a continuous sequence, when in fact the narrative covertly switches back to earlier matters which had been passed over. Failure to recognize the operation of this

123 rule leads to misunderstandings. It is said in Genesis: 'The

Lord God planted a garden in Eden to the east and placed there the man that he had made, and God also produced from the earth every tree that is beautiful to look at and good to eat' [Gen. 2: 8–9]. This gives the impression that the last action was done after he had made man and placed him in the garden, when in fact, having briefly mentioned both things—that God planted the garden and placed there the man that he had made—the writer recapitulates and goes back to say what he had passed over, namely how the garden was planted, and that 'God also produced from the earth every tree that is beautiful to look at and good to eat.' Finally, following this up, he added, 124 'and the tree of life in the middle of paradise and the tree of the knowledge of good and evil'. Then comes the river for the irrigation of the garden, divided into the four sources of the four rivers [Gen. 2: 9]: all this concerns the making of the garden. After finishing that description, the writer repeated what he had already said—and this really followed on at this point—in the words, 'And the Lord took the man that he had made and placed him in the garden' [Gen. 2: 15], and so on. For it was 125 after these actions that the man was placed there, as is now shown by the new order, and not the reverse, as its prior position in the narrative might lead one to think unless one was alert enough to recognize a recapitulation there, and a return to what had been passed over.

Similarly in the same book, where the generations of the 126 sons of Noah are recorded, it was said: 'These are the sons of Ham by their tribes, according to their tongues, by their lands, and by their races.' After the enumeration of the sons of Shem, it is said, 'These are the sons of Shem by their tribes, according to their tongues, by their lands, and by their races.' And then, referring to them all, the writer adds, 'These are the tribes of the sons of Noah, according to their generations and their races. From these tribes the various pockets of Gentiles were scattered over the earth after the flood. And every land had a single language, and all had one voice' [Gen. 10: 20, 10: 31–2, 11: 1]. This last addition, 'And every land had a single lan- 127 guage, and all had one voice' (that is, one common language), gives the impression that there was a single common language at the time when they had been dispersed over the land in

pockets of Gentiles. This is clearly inconsistent with the previous words, 'by their tribes and according to their languages'. Single tribes which had formed single races cannot be said to have had their own languages at a time when there was a single
128 language common to all. Therefore the words 'and every land had a single language, and all had one voice' are added by recapitulation, with the narrative covertly turning back on itself, in order to explain how it happened that after having a single common language they were divided among many. Immediately after this comes the story of the building of the tower; this was when the penalty for their arrogance was imposed on them by divine judgement. It was after this that they were scattered throughout the world according to their various languages [Gen. 11: 4–9].

129   This recapitulation may take an even more obscure form, as in the gospel where the Lord says, 'on the day that Lot left Sodom it rained fire from heaven and destroyed everyone: such will be the days of the Son of Man, when he is revealed. At that hour, if someone is on his roof and his goods in the house, he should not return to take them; and someone in the field likewise should not turn back. Remember Lot's wife' [Luke 17: 29–32]. Surely it is not at the time when the Lord is revealed that this advice is to be followed (not to look back, or, in other words, not to enquire into the past life which one has renounced), but rather at the present time, so that when the Lord is revealed one may find compensation for the things that
130 one has maintained or abandoned. But because of the words 'at that hour' it looks as if this advice is to be followed at the time when the Lord is revealed, unless the reader's senses are alert to the recapitulation. Help comes from another part of scripture, which proclaimed in the time of the apostles themselves, 'Sons, it is the last hour' [1 John 2: 18]. So it is the time in which the gospel is being preached, the time leading up to the revelation of the Lord, that is the hour at which that advice ought to be followed, because the actual revelation of the Lord relates to the time which will end with the day of judgement.

131   The seventh and last rule of Tyconius is 'On the devil and his body'. He is actually himself the head of the wicked, and they are, in a way, his body, destined to go with him into the

punishment of eternal fire [Matt. 25: 41], just as Christ is the head of the church [Eph. 1: 22–3], and the church is his body, destined to be with him in his kingdom in eternal glory. Just as the first rule ('On the Lord and his body') should make us alert, when scripture is speaking of one and the same person, to distinguish what applies to the head and what applies to the body, so here with the last: sometimes something is said against the devil which cannot be understood of him but rather concerns his body—a body which consists not only of those who are quite clearly outside [1 Cor. 5: 12], but also those who although they belong to him are nevertheless part of the church for the time being, until each individual departs this life and is separated out like chaff from wheat at the last judgement [Matt. 3: 12; Luke 3: 17]. The words of Isaiah, 'How Lucifer, son of the dawn, has fallen from the sky' [Isa. 14: 12] and the rest, which are spoken about, or to, one and the same person under the guise of the King of Babylon, are certainly in the actual context understood of the devil. But the following words, 'he who sends to all races is pounded into the earth', do not entirely apply to the head itself. It is true that the devil sends his angels to all races, yet it is the devil's body, not the devil himself, that is pounded into the earth, except in the sense that he is in his own body, which when pounded becomes dust for the wind to drive from the face of the earth [Ps. 1: 4]. 132

All these rules, with the single exception of the one entitled 'On the promises and the law', state that one thing is to be understood by another. This is the characteristic of metaphorical diction, which is too broad a category, it seems to me, to be comprehended in its entirety by a human being. Whenever one thing is said in order that something else may be understood, we have a metaphorical expression, even if the name of the actual trope is not found in the textbooks. When this takes a familiar form, understanding follows without effort; when it does not, effort is needed for understanding, and more in some cases than others, depending on the gifts of God bestowed on our human intellects or the assistance that he gives. As in the case of the literal usages that I discussed earlier, when things are to be understood in their plain sense, so too in metaphorical ones, expressed through tropes, when one thing must be 133

134

understood by another—which I have now dealt with at what seems appropriate length—students of our revered scriptures must be taught to recognize the various kinds of expression in holy scripture, to notice and memorize the ways in which it tends to say things, and especially—this is paramount, and absolutely vital—to pray for understanding. In the literature which they study they read that 'God gives wisdom, and from his face there is knowledge and understanding' [Prov. 2: 6], and it is from him too that they have received even their commitment to study, provided that it is accompanied by holiness.

135   But enough about signs, at least in their relation to words. It remains to present, in my next book, whatever the Lord prompts me to say on the subject of presenting our thoughts to others.

BOOK FOUR

In the initial arrangement of my material I divided this work of 1
mine, entitled *On Christian Teaching*, into two parts. After a
preface in which I answered those who were likely to criticize
this undertaking, I said, 'There are two things on which all
interpretation of scripture depends: the process of discovering
what we need to learn, and the process of presenting what we
have learnt. I shall discuss the process of discovery first, and
then that of presentation.'* Since I have already said a lot about 2
the former—making three volumes out of this single part—I
will now with the Lord's help say a little about presentation. If
possible, I will confine all my remarks to a single book and
bring this work to completion in four volumes.

At the outset I must curb the expectations of any readers 3
who think that I am going to present the rhetorical rules which
I learnt and taught in pagan schools, and warn them in this pre-
amble not to expect that sort of thing from me. This is not
because the rules have no practical use, but because such practical uses as they do have must be learnt separately—assuming
that a person of good character* has the time to learn them on
top of everything else—and not sought from me either in this
or any other work.

Since rhetoric is used to give conviction to both truth and 4
falsehood,* who could dare to maintain that truth, which
depends on us for its defence, should stand unarmed in the
fight against falsehood? This would mean that those who are
trying to give conviction to their falsehoods would know how
to use an introduction to make their listeners favourable, interested, and receptive, while we would not; that they would
expound falsehoods in descriptions that are succinct, lucid,
and convincing,* while we would expound the truth in such
a way as to bore our listeners, cloud their understanding, and
stifle their desire to believe; that they would assail the truth and
advocate falsehood with fallacious arguments, while we would
be too feeble either to defend what is true or refute what is
false; that they, pushing and propelling their listeners' minds

towards error, would speak so as to inspire fear, sadness, and elation, and issue passionate exhortations, while we, in the name of the truth, can only idle along sounding dull and indif-
5 ferent. Who could be so senseless as to find this sensible? No; oratorical ability, so effective a resource to commend either right or wrong, is available to both sides; why then is it not acquired by good and zealous Christians to fight for the truth, if the wicked employ it in the service of iniquity and error, to achieve their perverse and futile purposes?

6   As for the relevant observations and rules, which, together with a skilful manner of speaking that uses an abundance of words and verbal ornament, constitute what we mean by elo-quence,* these should be learnt independently of this work by those who can do so quickly, by setting aside an appropriate period of time at a suitable and convenient stage of their lives.
7 Even the luminaries of Roman eloquence were happy to say that if these things could not be learnt quickly they could never be properly learnt at all.* No need to ask whether this is true: for even if this subject could eventually be mastered by the less intelligent, I do not rate it so highly that I would wish people's
8 mature or advanced years to be devoted to learning it. It is enough if this task is left to young people, and not all those whom we desire to be educated for the good of the church, but those who are not yet bound by a more pressing responsibility or one with an unquestionably higher priority. Given a sharp and eager mind, eloquence is picked up more readily by those who read and listen to the words of the eloquent than by those
9 who follow the rules of eloquence. There is no shortage of Christian literature, even outside the canon* which has been raised to its position of authority for our benefit; and by read-ing this an able person, even one who is not seeking to become eloquent but just concentrating on the matters being dis-cussed, can become steeped in its eloquence, especially if this is combined with the practice of writing or dictating, and even-tually speaking, what is felt to be in conformity with the rule of
10 holiness and faith.* In the absence of such ability the rules of eloquence cannot be learnt, and even if they are laboriously drummed in and assimilated to some extent they are of no benefit. For even those who have learnt the rules and speak flu-

ently and stylishly are not all able to consider them as they speak in order to make sure that they are following them (unless of course they are discussing the actual rules). Indeed I think there are hardly any who are capable of doing both, that is, speaking well and considering as they speak the rules of eloquence which promote good speaking. There is a danger of 11 forgetting what one has to say while working out a clever way to say it. Yet we find the rules of eloquence observed in the sermons and addresses of eloquent men, even though the speakers—whether conversant with them or entirely untouched by them—did not consider them either when preparing to speak or when actually speaking. They observe the rules because they are eloquent; they do not use them to become eloquent.* Infants acquire speech purely by assimilating the words and 12 phrases of those who speak to them; so why should the eloquent not be able to acquire their eloquence not through the traditional teaching but by reading and listening to the speeches of the eloquent and by imitating them within the limits of their ability? Isn't this precisely what we see in practice? We know that there are very many speakers with no knowledge of rhetorical rules who are more eloquent than the many who have learnt them; but no one who has not read or listened to the disputations or addresses of good speakers is eloquent at all. Nor indeed would the art of grammar,* by which one is taught 13 to speak properly, be needed by children if it were possible for them to grow up and live their lives among people who spoke properly. Even though totally ignorant of the names of solecisms, they would, by virtue of their correct habits, note and avoid anything ungrammatical that they heard from any speaker, just as town-dwellers, even illiterate ones, find fault with country folk.

So the interpreter and teacher of the divine scriptures,* the 14 defender of the true faith and vanquisher of error, must communicate what is good and eradicate what is bad, and in this process of speaking must win over the antagonistic, rouse the apathetic, and make clear to those who are not conversant with the matter under discussion what they should expect. When he finds them favourable, interested, and receptive, or has made them so by his own efforts, then there are other goals to be

achieved, as the particular case demands. If listeners need information, there must be a presentation of the facts (if indeed this is really what is needed) to make the matter under discus-
15 sion more familiar. To clarify disputed issues there must be rational argument and deployment of evidence. But if listeners have to be moved rather than instructed, in order to make them act decisively on the knowledge that they have and lend their assent to matters which they admit to be true, then greater powers of oratory are required. In such cases what one needs is entreaties, rebukes, rousing speeches, solemn admonitions,* and all the other things which have the power to excite human emotions.

16   All these things that I have mentioned are continually being carried out by just about everybody in transactions per-
17 formed through speech. But since some performances are unintelligent, awkward, and boring, whereas others are clever, elegant, and exciting, the person required for the task under consideration is someone who can argue or speak wisely, if not eloquently. This will benefit his audience, albeit less so than if he could speak eloquently too. But the speaker who is awash with the kind of eloquence that is not wise is particularly dangerous because audiences actually enjoy listening to such a person on matters of no value to them, and reckon that some-body who is heard to speak eloquently must also be speaking
18 the truth. This point did not escape even those who believed in teaching the art of rhetoric; they declared that wisdom without eloquence was of little value to society but that eloquence with-out wisdom was generally speaking a great nuisance, and never beneficial.* If the writers of textbooks on rhetoric were forced by the pressure of the truth to admit this even in their books on the subject, notwithstanding the fact that they had no know-ledge of the true wisdom—the heavenly wisdom that comes down from the father of lights* [Jas. 1: 17]—how much more vital is it for us, the sons and servants of this wisdom, to hold the same opinion?

19   The wisdom of what a person says is in direct proportion to his progress in learning the holy scriptures—and I am not speaking of intensive reading or memorization, but real under-standing and careful investigation of their meaning. Some

people read them but neglect them; by their reading they profit in knowledge, by their neglect they forfeit understanding. Those who remember the words less closely but penetrate to 20 the heart of scripture with the eyes of their own heart are much to be preferred, but better than either is the person who not only quotes scripture when he chooses but also understands it as he should. For a person who has to speak wisely on matters 21 which he cannot treat eloquently, close adherence to the words of scripture is particularly necessary. The poorer he sees himself to be in his own resources, the richer he must be in those of scripture, using them to confirm what he says in his own words; so that although once deficient in words of his own he can grow in stature, as it were, by the testimony of something really important. A preacher who cannot give pleasure with his words may give pleasure with his texts. As for the person who 22 wants to speak eloquently as well as wisely—it will certainly be more beneficial if he can do both—I would be happier to refer him to eloquent speakers so that he can read their works, listen to their words, and practise imitating them, than to recommend that his time be spent on teachers of rhetoric, provided that those whom he will read and listen to are reliably said to be, or to have been, wise speakers as well as eloquent ones. Eloquent speakers give pleasure, wise ones salvation. That is 23 why scripture says not that 'a multitude of the eloquent . . .' but 'a multitude of the wise is the salvation of the world' [Wisd. 6: 26]. We often have to take bitter medicines, and we must always avoid sweet things that are dangerous: but what better than sweet things that give health, or medicines that are sweet? The more we are attracted by sweetness, the easier it is for medicine to do its healing work. So there are men of the church 24 who have interpreted God's eloquent utterances not only with wisdom but with eloquence as well;* and even for students with the leisure to read it is more likely that their time will run out than that these authors will be exhausted.

At this point someone may be asking whether the Christian 25 authors whose divinely inspired writings have created for us the canon of scripture with its most beneficial authority should be pronounced just wise, or eloquent as well. In my experience, and the experience of people who feel as I do on this matter, the question is a very easy one to answer. For when I understand these authors, not only can I conceive of nothing wiser; I can conceive of nothing more eloquent. Indeed, I venture to say that all who correctly understand what these writers are saying realize at the same time that it would not

26 have been right for them to express it in any other way. For just as there is one kind of eloquence appropriate to the young, and another kind appropriate to the old—and we should not call it eloquence if it does not match the status of the speaker—so there is a kind of eloquence appropriate to writers who enjoy the highest authority and a full measure of divine inspiration. They spoke in their own particular style, and it would be inappropriate for them to have used any other style, or for others to have used theirs. It is appropriate to them, and the humbler it seems, the more thoroughly it transcends that of others, not in

27 grandiloquence but in substance. When I fail to understand them, their eloquence is less clear, but I have no doubt that it is of the same standard as that which appears clearly when I do understand them. The fusion of obscurity with such eloquence in the salutary words of God was necessary in order that our minds could develop not just by making discoveries

28 but also by undergoing exertion.* If I had the time, I could exemplify, in the sacred literature of the writers that divine providence has supplied to educate us and lead us from this wicked world into the world of true happiness, all the qualities and figures of eloquence* which turn the heads of those who, on the basis not of grandeur but grandiloquence, prefer their

29 own style to that of Christian writers. But in that eloquence it is not the things which Christian writers have in common with pagan orators or poets that give me an inexpressible delight; what astonishes and overwhelms me is that they used our eloquence side by side with a rather different eloquence of their own in such a way that it is neither totally lacking nor unduly prominent in their writings. This is because it would have been wrong for it to be either discredited or paraded by the scriptures. (The first of these things would have happened if it had been completely avoided, the second, arguably, if it were easily

30 recognized.) In passages where scholars do perhaps recognize it, the subject-matter is such that the words used seem to be

ones not selected by the speaker but ones naturally associated with the actual topic. You could visualize it as wisdom proceeding from its own home (by this I mean a wise person's heart) and eloquence, like an ever-present slave, following on behind without having to be summoned.

In the following passage who can fail to see what the apostle 31 meant, and how wisely he expressed it? 'We rejoice in our sufferings, knowing that suffering produces endurance, and endurance character, and character hope, and that hope does not disappoint us; because God's love has been poured into our hearts through the Holy Spirit who has been given to us' [Rom. 5: 3–5]. Supposing that some unscholarly scholar of rhetoric (if I may put it like this) were to maintain that Paul had here followed rhetorical rules, surely he would be laughed out of court by educated and uneducated Christians alike? Yet we 32 recognize here the figure generally designated by the Greek word *climax*—though some prefer the Latin word *gradatio*,* not wishing to speak of a 'ladder'—whereby words or ideas are linked one with another. So here we see 'suffering' linked with 'endurance', 'endurance' linked with 'character', 'character' linked with 'hope'. Another ornament too may be recognized, whereby after certain sections, each articulated in a single phrase—these are known to Latin teachers as 'limbs' and 'pieces', but to Greeks as 'cola' and 'commata'—there follows an 'ambit' or 'circuit' (they call it a 'period'), in which the parts are left hanging by the speaker's voice until the period is completed by the last clause.* The first of the cola that precede 33 the period is 'that suffering produces endurance', the second is 'and endurance character', and the third 'and character hope'. Then comes the period itself, formed of three cola of which the first is 'and hope does not disappoint us', the second 'because God's love has been poured into our hearts', and the third 'through the Holy Spirit who has been given to us'. But these and other such things are part and parcel of traditional rhetoric. We do not say that Paul followed rhetorical rules; but neither do we deny that his wisdom was attended by eloquence.

In his second letter to the Corinthians, Paul refutes some 34 false apostles from the ranks of the Jews who were denigrating

him [2 Cor. 11: 16–30]. Obliged to blow his own trumpet, and
at the same time presenting this as foolishness, he spoke with
an amazing combination of wisdom and eloquence, but as the
servant of wisdom and the master of eloquence, being led
by the one but leading the other and not disdaining it as it
35 followed behind. 'I repeat,' he says, 'let nobody take me for a
fool; or if you do, then accept me as a fool, so that I too may
have my little boast. What I am saying I am saying not with the
Lord's authority, but as a fool, in this boastful confidence.
Since many people boast of worldly things, I will boast too. For
although wise yourselves, you gladly tolerate fools. You put up
with it if someone makes slaves of you, if someone preys on
you, if someone takes advantage of you, or puts on airs, or if
someone slaps you in the face. I speak in terms of embarrassment, as though I was made to look weak. But whatever anyone
dares to boast of (I am speaking as a fool), I dare to boast of it
too. Are they Hebrews? I am too. Are they Israelites? I am too.
Are they the seed of Abraham? I am too. Are they servants of
Christ? Speaking as a fool, I say I am even more so. I have been
many more times in adversity, more frequently in prison, the
victim of beatings without limit, and more often close to death.
Five times from the Jews I have received the thirty-nine lashes.
Three times I have been beaten with rods; once I was stoned;
three times I have suffered shipwreck; for a night and a day I
have been adrift on the open sea; often on the road, in danger
from rivers, in danger from robbers, in danger from my own
people, in danger from Gentiles, in danger in the city, in
danger in the desert, in danger at sea, in danger from false
brethren; suffering toil and hardship, and often deprived of
sleep; suffering hunger and thirst, and often without food;
and suffering from cold and exposure. And apart from those
external things, there is the daily pressure on me, my anxiety
for all my churches. Who is weakened, and I am not weak?
Who is made to stumble, and I am not bruised? If boasting
there must be, then I will boast of the things that show my
weakness.' The wisdom of these words is obvious to those who
are alert; the flood of eloquence which they combine to produce is apparent even to the inert.

36   A knowledgeable person recognizes that it is the above-

mentioned commata, cola, and periods that, deployed as they
are with tasteful variety, have produced all the beauty of this
style, which, like a pleasant face, pleases and moves even the
uneducated. Right from the beginning of the passage quoted 37
there are periods. The first is the smallest sort, one of two cola
(periods cannot have fewer than two,* but may have more): so
the first one is 'I repeat, let nobody take me for a fool'. Another,
of three cola, follows: 'or if you do, then accept me as a fool, so
that I too may have my little boast'. The third has four: 'What 38
I am saying I am saying not with the Lord's authority, but as a
fool, in this boastful confidence.' The fourth has two: 'Since
many people boast of worldly things, I will boast too.' The fifth
also has two: 'For although wise yourselves, you gladly tolerate
fools.' The sixth is also of two parts: 'You put up with it if
someone makes slaves of you.' Three commata follow: 'if
someone preys on you, if someone takes advantage of you, or
puts on airs'. Then there arc three cola: 'if someone slaps you 39
in the face. I speak in terms of embarrassment, as though I was
made to look weak.' A threefold period follows: 'But whatever
anyone dares to boast of (I am speaking as a fool), I dare to boast
of it too.' At this point three single commata reply individually
to three questions likewise expressed in three commata: 'Are
they Hebrews? I am too. Are they Israelites? I am too. Are they
the seed of Abraham? I am too.' A fourth comma, again in the
form of a question, receives a reply in the form not of another
comma, but a colon: 'Are they servants of Christ? Speaking as
a fool, I say I am even more so.' Then the series of questions is 40
tastefully withdrawn, and the four following commata pour
out: 'I have been many more times in adversity, more frequently in prison, the victim of beatings without limit, and
more often close to death.' Then a short period is added (it
must be marked by a pause in our articulation): 'Five times
from the Jews'—this is one comma, and it is joined by
another—'I have received the thirty-nine lashes.' Then he 41
reverts to commata, of which there are three: 'Three times I
have been beaten with rods; once I was stoned; three times I
have suffered shipwreck.' A colon follows: 'for a night and a
day I have been adrift on the open sea'. Next we have fourteen
commata, pouring out in a magnificent rush: 'often on the

road, in danger from rivers, in danger from robbers, in danger
from my own people, in danger from Gentiles, in danger in the
city, in danger in the desert, in danger at sea, in danger from
false brethren; suffering toil and hardship, and often deprived
of sleep; suffering hunger and thirst, and often without food;

42 and suffering from cold and exposure.' After this he adds a
period of three cola: 'And apart from those external things,
there is the daily pressure on me, my anxiety for all my
churches.' To this he adds two cola in the form of a question:
'Who is weakened, and I am not weak? Who is made to stumble, and I am not bruised?' Finally the whole of this rather
breathless passage is concluded with a bipartite period of two
cola: 'If boasting there must be, then I will boast of the things

43 that show my weakness.' After this blitz, by introducing a short
passage of narrative, he calms down, as it were, and makes the
reader calm down, with a grace and a charm that words cannot
adequately express. For he follows this up by saying: 'The God
and Father of the Lord Jesus, who is blessed for ever and ever,
knows that I am not lying.' And then he briefly describes how
he was in danger and how he escaped.

44   It would be tedious to examine all the passage's stylistic
virtues or to point them out in other passages of the holy scriptures. Suppose I had chosen to demonstrate the figures of
speech, as transmitted in textbooks of rhetoric, that occur just
in these passages, which I quoted to show Paul's eloquence:
serious men would think that I was overdoing it long before
any of those scholarly types thought that I had done enough.

45 When taught by schoolmasters all these things are regarded as
something great; they are bought at a great price, and sold with
great showmanship.* I am anxious to avoid giving the impression of showmanship in my discussion, but I had to reply to the
ill-educated people who think our authors contemptible not
because they do not possess the eloquence that our critics are so
inordinately fond of, but because they do not make a show of it.

46   But someone may be thinking that I chose the apostle Paul
just because he is the paragon of Christian eloquence. When he
said, 'Even if I am unskilled in speaking, I am not so in knowledge' [2 Cor. 11: 6], he appears to have been making a conces-
sion to his detractors rather than an acknowledgement of the

truth. If he had said, 'Unskilled in speech I may be, but not so in knowledge', there would be no other way to interpret it. Clearly he did not hesitate to admit his knowledge, without which he could not have been the teacher of the Gentiles. In any case, anything of his that we quote as a paradigm of 47 eloquence is taken from the letters, which even his detractors, who wanted him to be thought contemptible as a speaker, admitted to be weighty and powerful [2 Cor. 10: 10]. So I real- 48 ize that I must say something also about the eloquence of the prophets, in which much is obscure because of their figurative language. Indeed, the more opaque they seem, because of their use of metaphor, the greater the reader's pleasure when the meaning becomes clear. But I must make a similar analysis here, in passages where I am not obliged to explain the meaning but will restrict myself to presenting features of the style. I shall do this with particular reference to the book of the prophet who described himself as a shepherd or a herdsman, but was removed from that job by a divine summons and sent to prophesy to God's people. My text is not that of the Septuagint, whose seventy translators, though working with the help of the Holy Spirit, seem to have rendered some passages in different ways so that the reader's attention might be alerted to the search for spiritual meaning (which is why some of their sayings—the more figurative ones—are rather obscure), but that of the translation from Hebrew into Latin made by the priest Jerome,* an expert in both languages.

When condemning the wicked, the proud, and the self- 49 indulgent, and those who as a result were quite unmindful of brotherly love, this rustic (or erstwhile rustic) prophet exclaimed in these words [Amos 6: 1–6]: 'Woe to those of you who are comfortably off in Zion, and trust in the mountain of Samaria, leaders and heads of the peoples, who enter the house of Israel with pomp and circumstance! Go across to Calneh and see, and travel from there to Hamath the great and descend into Gath of the Philistines and to all their best kingdoms, to see if their territories are broader than your territories. You who are set apart for the day of evil and approach the throne of iniquity, who sleep on couches of ivory and run riot in your beds, who devour the lamb from the flock and calves from the

middle of the herd, who sing to the sound of the psaltery. Like
David, they thought that they had the vessels of song, drinking
wine in bowls, and anointed with the best perfume, and they
50 suffered no pain over the dismay of Joseph.' Would those who
despise our prophets as unlearned and unacquainted with eloquence (as if they themselves were learned and eloquent!) have
wished to speak any differently if they had had something
similar to say to such an audience—those of them, at any rate,
51 who did not want to behave like freaks? What is there that
discriminating ears could possibly want over and above such
eloquence? First, there is the invective, crashing with an
explosive roar upon sleepy senses to awaken them: 'Woe to
those of you who are comfortably off in Zion, and trust in the
mountain of Samaria, leaders and heads of the peoples, who
enter the house of Israel with pomp and circumstance!' Then
in order to show that because of their confidence in the mountain of Samaria (where idols were worshipped) they were
ungrateful for the benefits of God, who gave them the broad
expanses of their kingdom, he says: 'Go across to Calneh and
see, and travel from there to Hamath the great and descend
into Gath of the Philistines and to all their best kingdoms, to
52 see if their territories are broader than your territories.' As
these points are made, the discourse is enhanced, highlighted
as it were,* by the names of places—Zion, Samaria, Calneh,
Hamath the great, and Gath of the Philistines—and there is
elegant variation in the words attached to these place names:
'you are comfortably off', 'you trust', 'go across', 'travel',
53 'descend'. Their future enslavement under a wicked king is
aptly declared to be approaching in the following words: 'You
who are set apart for the day of evil and approach the throne of
iniquity'. Then the acts of self-indulgence follow: 'who sleep
on couches of ivory and run riot in your beds, who devour the
lamb from the flock and the calves from the middle of the
54 herd'. These six cola produce three bipartite periods.* He does
not say: 'You who are set apart for the day of evil, who
approach the throne of iniquity, who sleep on couches of ivory,
who run riot in your beds, who devour the lamb from the flock,
who devour the calves from the middle of the herd'; if he had,
this too would be attractively expressed, with all six cola each

flowing from the one repeated pronoun and each one marked off by a pause in the speaker's voice. But it was expressed more attractively by attaching to a single pronoun a pair of clauses, each of which expounded three ideas, one on the prediction of captivity ('who are set apart for the day of evil and approach the throne of iniquity'), one on their lust ('who sleep on couches inlaid with ivory, and run riot in your beds'), and the third on their greed ('who devour the lamb from the flock and calves from the middle of the herd'). So it is for the reader to choose whether to separate each element in pronunciation and make six cola, or, by not lowering the voice after the first, third, and fifth elements, to combine the first with the second, the third with the fourth, and the fifth with the sixth; he would thus, very tastefully, create three bipartite periods, of which one shows the impending disaster, one their sexual immorality, and one their extravagant gourmandise. Then he castigates the 55 self-indulgent pleasures of the ear. After saying 'who sing to the sound of the psaltery', he reins in the force of his invective with remarkable taste. He speaks not to them but about them and, in order to warn us to distinguish the wise man's music from the libertine's (for music can be performed wisely by the wise) does not say, 'who sing to the sound of the psaltery and like David think that you have the vessels of song'; but rather, 56 after saying something which these libertines needed to be told ('you who sing to the sound of the psaltery') he also somehow contrived to reveal their ignorance to others by adding, 'like David, they thought that they had the vessels of song, drinking wine in bowls, and anointed with the best perfume'. (These three cola are articulated better if the first two cola are not followed by a lowering of the voice and the period is rounded off by the third one.) Now for the phrase which is added to all this: 57 'and they suffered no pain over the dismay of Joseph'. Whether it is spoken continuously, as one colon, or, more tastefully, by lowering the voice after 'and they suffered no pain', and by adding the words 'over the dismay of Joseph' after a pause, creating a bipartite period, it is a sign of remarkable taste that he does not say, 'they suffered no pain over the dismay of their brother', but puts 'Joseph' instead of 'brother', so that any brother is signified by the proper name of the particular

brother whose fame, whether because of the injuries he suffered or the kindnesses with which he repaid them, over-
58 shadowed that of his brothers. I am not sure if the figure by
which 'Joseph' is made to stand for 'any brother' is specified in
the discipline which I learnt and taught;* but there is no need
to point out how attractive it is and how much it impresses
those who read and understand it to anyone if he does not
realize it for himself.

59   Even more things relevant to the rules of eloquence could be
discovered in this same passage which I quoted as an example.
But the effect of eloquence on a person of good character is not
so much to instruct when painstakingly discussed as to inspire
when passionately delivered. For such things were not produced by human labour, but poured from the divine mind with
both wisdom and eloquence; and it was not a case of wisdom
being devoted to eloquence but of eloquence keeping pace with
60 wisdom. As certain eloquent and discerning authorities were
able to see and say, the things that are learnt in the so-called art
of public speaking would not have been observed, noted, and
systematized into a discipline if they had not first been found in
the minds of orators;* so why be surprised if they are also
found in the words of men sent by God, the creator of all
minds? We should therefore acknowledge that our canonical
authors and teachers are eloquent, and not just wise, with a
kind of eloquence appropriate to the kind of persons they were.

61   Although I am taking numerous examples of style from
those of their writings which are understood without difficulty, we should certainly not think that they are suitable for
imitation in those passages where they have spoken with a
helpful and healthy obscurity in order to exercise and somehow refine their readers' minds or to overcome the reluctance
and whet the enthusiasm of those seeking to learn, or even in
order to cloud the minds of the wicked, whether this is done to
turn them to holiness or to exclude them from the holy mys-
62 teries. They spoke in this way so that later writers who understood and expounded them correctly might find within God's
church a further source of grace, one not equal to theirs but
subsidiary to it. Their expositors should not speak in such
a way that they set themselves up as similar authorities,

themselves in need of exposition, but should endeavour first
and foremost in all their sermons to make themselves understood and to ensure, by means of the greatest possible clarity,
that only the very slow fail to understand, and that the reason
why anything that we say is not easily or quickly understood
lies in the difficulty and complexity of the matters that we wish
to explain and clarify, and not in our mode of expression.
There are some things which are not understood, or barely 63
understood, in themselves, no matter how carefully they are
expressed or how many times they are repeated by even the
plainest of speakers. These things should seldom be put to a
popular audience, and then only if there is a pressing need, or
arguably never at all. But in the case of books, which because
they are in writing somehow grip the reader when they are
understood, and do not annoy people when they are not understood, if they really want to read them, and also in the case of
debates with certain sorts of people, we should not shirk the
duty of making plain to the minds of others the truths which
we have ourselves perceived, however hard they may be to
comprehend, with as much effort and argument as may be
necessary; always assuming that our listener or disputant has
the will to learn and does not lack the mental capacity to absorb
such things, in whatever way they are presented by a teacher
concerned not for the eloquence of his teaching but its clarity.

The careful pursuit of this clarity sometimes leads one to 64
neglect elegant vocabulary and consider not what sounds good
but what is good for putting over and making clear what
one has to say. One writer, when dealing with this kind of
discourse, spoke of a 'contrived casualness'.* Such a style dis-
poses of ornament without exposing itself to squalor. But good 65
teachers take, or should take, the greatest care to ensure that a
word which cannot be good Latin unless it is obscure or
ambiguous, but which is used in colloquial speech in a way that
avoids obscurity and ambiguity, is not used as it is used by educated people but rather as the uneducated tend to use it. Our
translators were happy to say 'I shall not convene assemblies
from their bloods'* [Ps. 15: 4 (16: 4)], since they realized that it
was important in this particular context to use the plural form
of this noun, although it is used only in the singular in Latin; so

why should a teacher of holiness, when speaking to the unlearned, be averse to saying *ossum* rather than *os*, so as to prevent the monosyllable being interpreted not as the singular of *ossa* but as the singular of *ora* (since the African ear is not a good

66 judge of long or short vowels)? What is the use of correct speech if it does not meet with the listener's understanding? There is no point in speaking at all if our words are not understood by the people to whose understanding our words are directed. The teacher, then, will avoid all words that do not communicate; if, in their place, he can use other words which are intelligible in their correct forms, he will choose to do that, but if he cannot—either because they do not exist or because they do not occur to him at the time—he will use words that are less correct, provided that the subject-matter itself is communicated and learnt correctly.

67 This aim of being intelligible should be strenuously pursued not only in debates, whether with one person or several, but also, and this is even more important, in public gatherings when a sermon is delivered. In debates everyone has an opportunity to ask questions, but when all hush their voices to listen to one speaker, and turn their attentive faces towards him, it is not usual or acceptable for someone to ask questions about something he has not understood. So the speaker's sensitivity

68 must come to the aid of the silent listener. A crowd that is eager to learn tends to show by its movements whether it has understood. Until it does show this, the topic must be rolled around in a variety of different ways—this is not possible for those who deliver prepared or memorized speeches—but when it is clear that it has been understood, the sermon should be brought to an end or a transition made to another topic.

69 A speaker who clarifies something that needs to be learnt is a blessing, but a speaker who labours things already learnt is a bore, at least for those who were keyed up by the prospect of resolving difficulties in the matters being explained. But in order to delight one's audience even well-known topics may be treated; here the attraction lies not in the topics themselves, but in the style. If this is itself familiar and welcome to an audience, it hardly matters whether the speaker speaks extempore

70 or reads his speech. Things which are well written tend not

only to be read with pleasure on first acquaintance, but also to be reread with considerable pleasure by those who are already acquainted with and have not yet lost their memory of them; and both classes tend to enjoy listening to them. (When a person is reminded of something he has forgotten, he is being taught.*) But I am not now concerned with methods of giving pleasure; I am speaking about methods of teaching people who are eager to learn. The best method is one by which the listener 71 hears the truth and understands what he hears. Once this goal has been reached there is no need to busy oneself in teaching that particular topic any longer, but it may be necessary to make it attractive, and so implant it in the mind. If this does seem necessary, it should be done with restraint, to prevent boredom.

In a word, the function of eloquence in teaching is not to 72 make people like what was once offensive, or to make them do what they were loth to do, but to make clear what was hidden from them. If this is done in a disagreeable way, the benefits reach only a few enthusiasts, who are eager to know the things they need to learn no matter how dull and unattractive the teaching may be. Once they have attained it, they feed on the truth itself with great delight; it is the nature of good minds to love truth in the form of words, not the words themselves. What use is a golden key, if it cannot unlock what we want to be 73 unlocked, and what is wrong with a wooden one, if it can, since our sole aim is to open closed doors? Learning has a lot in common with eating: to cater for the dislikes of the majority even the nutrients essential to life must be made appetizing.

It has been said by a man of eloquence, and quite rightly, 74 that the eloquent should speak in such a way as to instruct, delight, and move their listeners.* He then added: 'instructing is a matter of necessity, delighting a matter of charm, and moving them a matter of conquest'. The first of these three, the need to instruct, relates to the subject-matter of our discourse, the other two to the style we use. A speaker wishing to instruct should not think that he has communicated what he wishes to communicate to the person he wishes to instruct until he is understood. Even if he has said what he himself understands, he should not yet think that he has communicated with the

person who fails to understand him; but if he has been understood, then, no matter how he has spoken, he has communi
75 cated. But if he also wishes to delight the person he is speaking to, or to move him, he will not achieve this by speaking anyhow; it makes a difference what style he uses for this purpose. A hearer must be delighted so that he can be gripped and made to listen, and moved so that he can be impelled to action. Your hearer is delighted if you speak agreeably, and moved if he values what you promise, fears what you threaten, hates what you condemn, embraces what you commend, and rues the thing which you insist that he must regret, and if he rejoices at what you set forth in your preaching as something joyful, pities those whom by your words you present to his mind's eye as miserable, and shuns those whom with terrifying language you urge him to avoid. There are other things too in this grand style of eloquence which can be done to move the minds of listeners, the purpose being not to make known to them what they must do, but to make them do what they already know must be done.
76 If they are still ignorant, they must of course be instructed rather than moved. And perhaps when they know the relevant facts they will be moved to such a degree that greater powers of eloquence are not needed to move them. But this must be done when necessary; and it is necessary when although they know they must do something they fail to do it. This is why instruction is a matter of necessity. People may either do or not do what they know must be done; but who could say that they must do something which they do not know they must do? The reason why moving people is not a matter of necessity is that it is not always needed, as when a listener assents to a speaker who is merely instructing or perhaps also delighting him. The reason why it is a matter of conquest is that it is possible for a
77 person to be instructed and delighted but not give assent. What use would the first two be without the third? Nor is giving delight a matter of necessity, since when truths are being demonstrated by a speaker—this relates to the task of instruction—it is not the aim of the eloquence or the intention of the speaker that the truths or the eloquence should in themselves produce delight; but the truths themselves, as they are revealed, do produce delight by virtue of being true. Similarly

the exposure and refutation of falsehoods generally give delight. They do not give delight because they are false, but because it is true that they are false delight is given by the words in which this truth is demonstrated.

Because of the disdainful kind of person who is not satisfied 78 by the truth presented anyhow, but accepts it only if expressed in such a way that the discourse also gives pleasure, delight has been given an important role in eloquence. But even the extra contribution of this is not enough for the hard-hearted, who stand to gain neither from mere understanding nor from their delight in the teacher's style. How do those two things benefit a person who admits the truth and praises the style but does not give his assent—which is the whole point of the speaker's tire-less concentration on the subject-matter of his address when advocating a particular course of action? If one is giving 79 instruction on the sort of topic in which belief or knowledge is sufficient, consent is nothing more than the acknowledgement that what is said is true. But when one is giving instruction about something that must be acted on, and one's aim is to pro-duce this action, it is futile to persuade people of the truth of what is being said, and futile to give delight by the style one uses, if the learning process does not result in action. So when advocating something to be acted on the Christian orator should not only teach his listeners so as to impart instruction, and delight them so as to hold their attention, but also move them so as to conquer their minds. The kind of listener that 80 still has to be moved to give his consent by a grand style of eloquence is one in which this end has not been achieved by the demonstration of the truth—even if this leads to the open acknowledgement of it—in combination with a charming style.

So much attention has been paid to the charms of style that 81 not only things which should not be done but even things which should be avoided and abhorred—evil and wicked things, eloquently advocated by evil and wicked men—are avidly read about by people without any intention of giving their consent but simply for the sake of delight. May God keep from his church the attitude described by Jeremiah when he says of the Jewish synagogue: 'Fearful and terrible things have

happened in the land. The prophets were prophesying
iniquity and the priests have given applause with their hands
and my people have loved it so. And what will you do in the
82 time to come?' [Jer. 5: 30–1]. What eloquence—all the more
terrifying for its directness, and all the more compelling for its
steadfastness! It is indeed the 'axe which shatters rocks' [Jer.
23: 29], to which God himself, in the words of this very
prophet, compared the word which he proclaimed through his
holy prophets. Be it far, far from us, that priests should
83 applaud speakers of iniquity, and God's people love it so. May
such madness be far from us, I say; for what shall we do in the
time to come? And indeed let what is spoken be less well
understood, less delightful, and less moving, as long as the
truth be spoken and justice, not iniquity, be what gives listeners pleasure. That certainly cannot be the case if it is not pre-
84 sented attractively. But a serious congregation, about which
the Psalmist said to his God, 'I shall praise you in a serious congregation' [Ps. 34: 18 (35: 18)], will not even take delight in the
attractive style that is devoted not to presenting iniquity but to
enhancing trivial and ephemeral goods with the sort of osten-
tatious verbal froth which could not even enhance important
and lasting things in a tasteful and serious way. There is something of the sort in a letter of the blessed Cyprian, and I think it
was allowed to happen, or done on purpose, so that posterity
might know that his style was rescued from this exuberance by
the soundness of his Christian teaching and confined to a more
serious and modest kind of eloquence, like that of his later
letters, which is freely enjoyed and diligently imitated but
85 matched only with the greatest difficulty. He says in one
passage [*Ep.* 1]: 'Let us seek this bower; the nearby solitudes
offer seclusion, where, with the wandering shoots of the vine
branches creeping with their pendulous clusters across their
supporting trellises, the leafy roofs have created a vine-clad
colonnade.' This is spoken with a marvellously extravagant
profusion of verbal riches, but offends serious minds by its
86 excessive elaboration. Admirers of this style believe that people who do not speak like this, but express themselves more
severely, are incapable of such writing, not that they deliberately avoid it. So this holy man has shown not only that he

could speak in this way, because he did so in one passage, but also that he preferred not to, because after this he did so nowhere else.

The aim of our orator, then, when speaking of things that 87 are just and holy and good—and he should not speak of anything else—the aim, as I say, that he pursues to the best of his ability when he speaks of these things is to be listened to with understanding, with pleasure, and with obedience. He should be in no doubt that any ability he has and however much he has derives more from his devotion to prayer than his dedication to oratory; and so, by praying for himself and for those he is about to address, he must become a man of prayer before becoming a man of words. As the hour of his address approaches, before he opens his thrusting lips he should lift his thirsting soul to God so that he may utter what he has drunk in and pour out what has filled him. On any one of the subjects which must be 88 treated in terms of faith and love there are many points to make, and many ways for those who know about these things to make them; who can know what it is expedient for us to say or our audience to hear at a particular moment but the one who sees the hearts of all? And who can ensure that we say what is right and say it in the right way but the one 'in whose hands we, and our sermons, exist' [Wisd. 7: 16]? So let the person who 89 wishes both to know and to teach learn everything that he needs to teach, and acquire the skill in speaking appropriate to a Christian orator; but nearer the time of his actual address let him consider that there is more suitable advice for a holy mind in what the Lord says: 'Do not worry about what to say or how to say it; for you will be given words to speak when the time comes. For it is not you who speak, but the Spirit of your Father who speaks within you' [Matt. 10: 19–20]. If the Holy Spirit speaks in those who are delivered to their persecutors for Christ's sake, why should he not also speak in those who deliver Christ to their pupils?

Anyone who says that there is no need to give people 90 instruction about what, or how, to teach, if it is the Holy Spirit that makes men teachers, may as well say that there is no need for us to pray, since the Lord says, 'Your Father knows what you need before you ask him' [Matt. 6: 8]; or that the apostle

Paul should not have instructed Timothy and Titus on what or how to teach others. (A person who has been given the position of teacher in the church should keep these three apostolic
91 letters before his eyes.) In 1 Timothy we read, 'Pass on these things and teach them' [1 Tim. 4: 11]. (What they are has been mentioned earlier.) We also find there: 'Do not chide an elder, but appeal to him as you would to your father' [1 Tim. 5: 1]. In the second letter he is told, 'Stick to the form of sound words that you heard from me' [2 Tim. 1: 13]. He is also told, 'Do your best to show yourself to God as a reliable workman with no need to be ashamed, rightly handling the word of truth' [2 Tim. 2: 15]. There is also the advice, 'Preach the word, insist on it at times convenient and inconvenient; criticize, encourage, and reprimand with all possible persistence and teaching'
92 [2 Tim. 4: 2]. And again, he tells Titus that a bishop must be resolute in teaching the infallible word 'so that he may be strong in sound teaching and able to refute those who speak against it' [Titus 1: 9], and also: 'But you must say what befits sound teaching, that old men must be sober' [Titus 2: 1–2], and so on. And this too: 'Speak these things, and give encouragement and reprimand with all authority. Let nobody despise you. Remind them to be submissive to rulers and authorities'
93 [Titus 2: 15–3: 1], and so on. So what is our verdict? Surely the apostle is not in two minds when he says that teachers are made by the working of the Holy Spirit but also gives instruction about what and how they should teach? Or are we rather to understand two things at once—that through the abundant gifts of the Holy Spirit the human task of teaching even the teachers themselves must not cease, and that 'neither the one who plants nor the one who waters is anything, but it is God
94 who produces the growth'? [1 Cor. 3: 7]. That is why even with the ministry of holy men, or indeed the co-operation of the holy angels, nobody properly learns the things that appertain to a life with God, unless, through God, he becomes responsive to God, to whom it is said in the Psalm: 'Teach me to do your will, since you are my God' [Ps. 142: 10 (143: 10)]. That is why the apostle says to Timothy himself, speaking as teacher to disciple, 'You must be resolute in the things you have learnt and which have been passed on to you, knowing from whom

you have learnt them' [2 Tim. 3: 14]. Physical medicines, 95
applied by humans to other humans, only benefit those in
whom the restoration of health is effected by God, who can
heal even without them (but they cannot work without him,
yet are applied all the same); and if this is done conscientiously,
it is reckoned as a work of mercy or kindness. So too the benefits of teaching, applied to the soul through human agency, are
only beneficial when the benefit is effected by God, who could
have given the gospel to man even without human writers or
intermediaries [cf. Gal. 1: 11–12].

So the speaker who is endeavouring to give conviction to 96
something that is good should despise none of these three
aims—of instructing, delighting, and moving his hearers—
and should make it his prayerful aim to be listened to with
understanding, with pleasure, and with obedience, as I have
stated above. If he does this properly and appropriately he can
fairly be called eloquent, even if he does not meet with his audience's assent. It appears that the selfsame authority on Roman
eloquence wanted to relate these three aims—of instructing,
delighting, and moving an audience—to the following three
styles, when, in a similar way, he said: 'So the eloquent speaker
will be one who can treat small matters in a restrained style,
intermediate matters in a mixed style, and important matters
in a grand style.'* It is as if he were adding this triad to the
first one and so forming a single coherent statement like this:
'The eloquent speaker will be one who can treat small matters
in a restrained style in order to instruct, intermediate matters
in a mixed style in order to delight, and important matters in a
grand style in order to move an audience.'

He could have exemplified these three styles, as used by 97
him, in forensic cases, but not in our matters, that is the ecclesiastical matters which will engage the speaker of whom I am
offering a sketch. In forensic cases small matters in their terms
are ones in which judgement must be made on financial questions, and great matters are ones in which human life is at stake;
whereas matters in which none of these things is at issue, and
the aim is not action or decision, but solely the delight of the
listener, have been called intermediate (as falling between the
two) and so moderate, or limited: the word 'moderate' derives

from the word *modus* ['limit']. (When we use this word in the
98 sense of 'small' we are using it loosely, not literally.) But in our
situation, since we must relate everything, especially what we
say to congregations from our position of authority, to the
well-being of human beings not in this temporary life but in
eternity, where there is the added danger of eternal perdition,
all matters that we speak of are important, so much so that not
even what a Christian teacher says about acquiring or losing
sums of money should be thought of as a small matter, whether
99 the amount is big or little. For justice, which we must certainly
observe even in small financial transactions, is not a small matter: as the Lord says, 'The person who is trustworthy in small
matters is trustworthy in important ones too' [Luke 16: 10]. A
small matter is small; but to be trustworthy in a small matter is
something important. Just as the property of roundness—by
virtue of which all lines drawn from the centre of a circle to its
circumference are equal—is the same in a large dish as in the
tiniest coin, so the importance of justice is not diminished
when small matters are performed with justice.

100   When speaking about secular lawsuits (meaning of course
financial ones) the apostle Paul said [1 Cor. 6: 1–9], 'Does any
of you who has a dispute with another dare to be judged by the
wicked, and not before the holy? Do you not know that the holy
will judge the world? And if the world is judged by you, are you
unworthy to pass judgement on small matters? Do you not
know that, far from secular business, we shall judge angels? So
if you have secular disputes, take as your judges those who are
despised in the church! I say this to awaken your self-respect.
Is there among you no wise man who could judge between the
brethren? But brother passes judgement on brother, and that
before unbelievers. Now it is really culpable of you to have lawsuits against each other. Why not rather accept injustice? Why
not rather be defrauded? But you are perpetrating injustice
and fraud: and this against your own brethren. Do you not
know that the unjust will not inherit the kingdom of God?'
101 What was it that made him so indignant that he rebukes,
reproaches, reprimands, and threatens like this? What was it
that made him show his inner feelings with such frequent and
violent changes in his voice? And why is it that he speaks so

grandly about small matters? Did human business deserve so much of his attention? Far from it. He did all this in the interests of justice, love, and holiness, which as no sensible mind can doubt are important even in the smallest issues. Now if we 102 were advising men how to conduct secular cases before church courts, for themselves or for their families, we would certainly be right to advise them to deal with small matters in a restrained style. But since we are discussing the discourse of the man whom we wish to be a teacher of those things by which we are freed from eternal ills and attain eternal well-being, wherever they may be raised—whether in public or in private, whether with one person or several, whether with friends or opponents, whether in continuous speech or in debate, whether in treatises or in books, whether in letters of great length or extreme brevity—they are important.

Unless of course we think that because a cup of cold water is 103 a trivial and valueless thing the Lord is saying something trivial and valueless when he declares that the person who gives a cup to one of his disciples will not lose his reward [Matt. 10: 42]? Or that when a teacher in church bases a sermon on this he should consider himself to be speaking of something small, and so speak not in the intermediate or the grand style, but the restrained style? Is it not true that on one occasion when I happened to be speaking on this before a congregation and God by his presence enabled me to speak suitable words, there somehow arose from that cold water a flame to fire the cold hearts of men to perform works of mercy in the hope of heavenly reward?

But although our teacher must be a speaker on important 104 matters, he should not always speak of them in the grand style, but rather use the restrained style when teaching and the intermediate style when censuring or praising something. But when action must be taken and we are addressing those who ought to take it but are unwilling, then we must speak of what is important in the grand style, the style suitable for moving minds to action. Sometimes one speaks about one and the same important matter in all three styles: in the restrained style, if it is being taught; in the moderate style, if it is being praised; and in the grand style, if antagonistic minds are being driven to

105 change their attitude. What is greater than God himself? But
does that mean he is not the subject of teaching? Surely a
speaker teaching the unity of the Trinity should keep exclusively to the restrained style in order to make this difficult and
complicated matter as comprehensible as he can? Surely it is
not the case that ornament rather than argument is required, or
that the reader needs to be moved in the interests of action
106 rather than instructed in the interests of edification? And when
God is being praised, either in himself or in his works, what a
display of attractive and brilliant oratory appears in the mouth
of the preacher who can praise God as far as is possible—for
nobody praises God adequately yet nobody fails to praise him
in some way! And if God is not worshipped, or if idols or
demons or any other created things are worshipped alongside
him or in his place, the enormity of this evil, and the necessity
for men to turn away from such an evil, must certainly be
expressed in the grand style.

107   There is an example of the restrained style in the apostle
Paul—to take one of the clearer instances—where he says
[Gal. 4: 21–6]: 'Tell me, you who wish to be under the law, do
you not listen to the law? It is written that Abraham had two
sons, one by a slave and one by a free woman; the son of the
slave was born according to the flesh, but the son of the free
woman through God's promise. This is an allegory. These are
in fact the two covenants: one, from Mount Sinai, by which
people are born into slavery—this is Hagar. Sinai is a mountain
in Arabia, which corresponds to the present Jerusalem; she is
in slavery along with her sons. But the heavenly Jerusalem is
108 the free woman, and she is our mother', and so on. Similarly,
where he is reasoning, and says [Gal. 3: 15–18]: 'Brethren, here
is a human example. A human covenant, once ratified, cannot
be made void or added to by anyone. The promises were made
to Abraham and his offspring. He does not say "offsprings",
meaning several, but "and to your offspring, which is Christ",
meaning one. My point is this: the covenant ratified by God is
not undermined, or the promises nullified, by a law made four
hundred and thirty years later. For if the inheritance comes by
law, it does not come by promise; but God bestowed it on
109 Abraham by promise.' And because he was able to meet the

objection, 'Why then was the law given, if inheritance does not come through it?', he raised this objection himself, saying in the form of a question [Gal. 3: 19], 'What then is the point of the law?', and then replied: 'It was promulgated because of wrongdoing, until the arrival of the offspring to which the promise was made; and this was arranged through angels by the agency of an intermediary. An intermediary does not exist for one party alone, and God is one' [Gal. 3: 19–20]. Here too something occurred to him, and he presented it himself: 'Is the law then at odds with God's promises?' 'Far from it', is his reply, followed by the explanation, 'Had we been given a law capable of giving life, then righteousness would certainly come through law. But scripture has subjected everything to the rule of sin in order that the promise might be given to believers through faith in Jesus Christ' [Gal. 3: 21–2]. And there is more in this vein. So it is part of the teacher's task not just to reveal 110 what is hidden and solve knotty problems but also, while doing this, to anticipate other questions which may arise, in case they undermine or refute what we are saying; provided, of course, that the solution also presents itself to us, so that we do not undermine our sure foundation. It tends to happen that one question leads to others, and these in turn lead to yet more, and that as these are investigated and answered the thread of our argument becomes so extended that unless endowed with a very good memory the debater is unable to return to his starting-point. But it is a very good idea to refute something that can be refuted, if an argument presents itself, in case it presents itself either in a situation where there is nobody able to answer it or in the mind of someone who is present at the meeting but keeps quiet, and consequently goes away unenlightened.

The mixed style is found in the following words of Paul 111 [1 Tim. 5: 1–2]: 'Do not rebuke an older man, but appeal to him as you would to a father. Treat younger men as brothers, old ladies as mothers, and young girls as sisters.' And in these too [Rom. 12: 1]: 'I appeal to you, brethren, by the mercy of God, to present your bodies as a sacrifice which is living, holy, and acceptable to God.' Indeed just about the whole of this exhortation exemplifies the mixed style of speaking. The most attractive parts are those in which there is a graceful flow of

phrases each duly balanced by other phrases, as here [Rom.
112 12: 6–16]: 'We have various gifts, to be used according to the particular grace bestowed on us: prophecy, to be used according to
the rule of faith; or service, to be used in our ministry; or, if one
teaches, in teaching; or if one exhorts, in exhortation; or, if one
is a giver, in wholehearted generosity; or if one is a leader, with
a sense of responsibility; or if one shows mercy, with a spirit of
cheerfulness. Let your love be without pretence; hate evil, and
stick to what is good, loving one another with brotherly love,
outdoing one another in mutual respect, unremitting in enthusiasm, fervent in spirit, serving the Lord, rejoicing in hope,
patient in suffering, constant in prayer, contributing to the
needs of the saints, practising hospitality. Bless those that persecute you, bless rather than curse. Rejoice with those that
rejoice, weep with those that weep, having the same feelings as
113 each other.' Attractive too is the way in which this whole out-
pouring of words is concluded with a period of two cola: 'not
having haughty ideas, but associating with the humble'. And a
little later he says [Rom. 13: 6–8]: 'Persevering in this very
thing, give to all what is their due: tribute, if it is tribute; tax, if
it is tax; respect, if it is respect; honour, if it is honour.' These
words, arranged in cola, are themselves concluded by a period,
consisting of two cola: 'owe nothing to anyone except the duty
of mutual love'. And a little later he says [Rom. 13: 12–14]:
'The night is far gone, and the day is at hand. So let us throw
off the works of darkness and put on the armour of light. Let us
behave honourably, as in the day, not in revels and drunken-
ness, not in debauchery and vice, not in quarrelling and jealousy. Put on the Lord Jesus Christ, and do not give thought to
114 the flesh by indulging passionate desires.' If this had been put
in the following way, 'Do not, by indulging passionate desires,
give thought for the flesh', the more rhythmical sentence-
ending would doubtless have been more pleasing to the ear;
but the serious-minded translator preferred to retain the exact
word-order. Suitably advanced scholars of Greek rhetoric may
investigate how it sounds in Greek, the language that the apostle used; but to me the version that we have in Latin, keeping to
the original word-order, does not seem very rhythmical either.
115 It must certainly be admitted that the stylistic embellishment

that derives from rhythmical clausulae is missing in the Latin scriptures. Whether this is the fault of the translators or whether (as I suspect is more likely) they deliberately avoided such specious things, I do not venture to say: I admit I do not know. But this I do know, that if an expert in prose rhythm were to produce clausulae according to the rules that govern such rhythm—this could be done very easily by substituting certain words which have the same meaning, or by changing the order of the words found in the text—he would discover that these divinely inspired writers lack none of those supposedly important features which he learnt in the schools of grammar and rhetoric; he would also find many types of elegant expression—elegant in our language, certainly, but particularly so in the original—none of which is found in the literature which fills them with such pride. But there is a dan- 116
ger of reducing the weight of the impressive divine writings while enhancing the rhythm. Our prophets were not ignorant of music, the subject which gives the fullest instruction in rhythm, and indeed the learned Jerome mentions the metres used by some of them,* in the Hebrew, but in the interests of verbal accuracy he did not reproduce them in his translation. If 117
I may state my own attitude—which is of course better known to me than it is to other people, and better known to me than the attitudes of other people—I do not neglect clausular rhythm in my own speaking, but apply it in what I consider to be moderation; and in our writers they have extra appeal because I find them so rarely.

What especially differentiates the grand style from the 118
mixed style is that it is not so much embellished with verbal ornament as inflamed by heartfelt emotion. It has room for almost all those ornaments, but if they are not there they are not missed. It is borne along by its own momentum, and derives its beauty of expression, if indeed this emerges, from the power of its subject-matter, and not the pursuit of elegance. It is sufficiently equipped for its purpose if appropriate words follow not from a search for elaborate vocabulary but from the promptings of a passionate heart. If a brave man 119
happens to be armed with a golden and bejewelled sword, it is not because his weapon is precious that he does what he does

with it in the heat of battle but because it is a weapon; and he remains the same mighty warrior even when 'anger makes a weapon of whatever his groping search supplies'.* In the following passage [2 Cor. 6: 2–11] the apostle pleads that in the service of the gospel the evils of the present time should all be endured with the support of God's gifts. An important subject, it is treated in the grand style, and not without ornament.

120   'Behold,' he says, 'now is the acceptable time, behold, now is the day of salvation. We give no offence in anything, lest our ministry incur blame, but commend ourselves in everything as the servants of God, in great endurance, in afflictions, in hardships, in crises, in beatings, in imprisonments, in riots, in labours, in sleepless nights, in hunger, in purity, in knowledge, in long-suffering, in kindness, in the Holy Spirit, in genuine love which is not feigned, in the word of truth, in the power of God, through the weapons of justice on the left hand and on the right, through glory and dishonour, through bad repute and good repute, as impostors and yet truthful, as men who are unknown and yet known, as dying, and (behold) yet alive, as punished yet not put to death, as sorrowful yet always rejoicing, as needy but enriching many, as if owning nothing yet possessing everything.' And notice the impassioned sequel: 'Our mouth is open to you, Corinthians, our heart is wide,' and the rest, which it would take a long time to give in full.

121   Similarly, when writing to the Romans [Rom. 8: 28–39] he pleads that the persecutions of this world be overcome through love, with an assured hope in the assistance of God. He pleads in a style both grand and ornate: 'We know that for those who love God all things work together for good, for those who are called according to his purpose. For those that he foreknew he also predestined to be conformed to the image of his son, so that he might be the first-born of many brothers. Those that he predestined, he also called; and those that he called, he also justified; and those that he justified, he also glorified. So what shall we say to all this? If God is for us, who is against us? Since he did not spare his own son, but delivered him for the good of us all, how can he fail to give us all things together with him? Who will make an accusation against God's elect? God, who justifies? Who is there who condemns us? Christ Jesus, who

died, and what is more rose again, and is indeed at the right hand of God, actually interceding for us? Who will separate us from the love of Christ? Will affliction? Distress? Hunger? Nakedness? Danger? Violence? As it is written, "For your sake we are being done to death all day long, we have been reckoned as sheep for the slaughter" [Ps. 43: 22 (44: 22)]. But in all these things we are more than conquerors through the one that loved us. For I am certain that neither death nor life, neither angel nor emperor, neither present nor future, nor power, nor height, nor depth, nor any other creature, will be able to separate us from the love of God which is in Christ Jesus our Lord.'

In Galatians, although the whole letter is written in the 122 restrained style except for the last part, where the mixed style is used, he inserts a passage of such powerful emotion that although lacking any of the ornaments that we found in the passages quoted above it can only be assigned to the grand style. He says [Gal. 4: 10–20]: 'You observe days and months 123 and years and seasons. I fear that perhaps I have laboured for you in vain. Be as I am, just as I became like you. Brethren— I implore you—you have done me no injury. You know that it was through physical weakness that I preached the gospel to you long ago, and you know that you did not despise or shrink from the trials that you had over my physical condition but welcomed me like an angel of God, like Christ Jesus. How great was your happiness! I bear witness to you, that had it been possible you would have torn out your own eyes and given them to me. So have I become your enemy by preaching the truth to you? They are envious of you, but not with an honest envy; they want to exclude you, so that you will envy them. It is a good thing to feel envy, but always in an honest matter, and not only when I am present with you. My dear sons, with whom I am once again in labour, until Christ is formed in you—I wish I could now be present among you and change my tone. I am amazed at you.' Clearly there are here no pairs of 124 words or phrases in stylistic opposition, no words joined one to another to form a climax,* and no euphonious cola, or commata, or periods; but that does not imply a cooling of the great emotion which makes his discourse boil over with passion.

But these sayings of Paul, although clear, are also profound, 125 and although written down and widely known require not only a reader or listener but also an expositor, if somebody is not content with the surface meaning but seeks to probe their depths. So let us look at these styles in writers who by their reading of scripture attained a knowledge of the divine truths of salvation and made it available to the church. The blessed Cyprian uses the restrained style in the treatise in which he 126 discusses the sacrament of the cup. Here he is answering the question whether the Lord's cup should hold water alone, or water mixed with wine. A part of this should be quoted as an example. After the beginning of the letter, as he begins to answer the question he has raised, he says [Cypr. *Ep*. 63. 2–4], 'You should know that we were instructed to follow the Lord's teaching in the offering of the cup and not to do anything except what the Lord, on our behalf, did first; it follows that the cup offered in remembrance of him should be offered with an admixture of wine. Since Christ says, "I am the true vine" [John 15: 1], the blood of Christ is surely not water but wine. Nor is it possible for his blood, by which we have been redeemed and made alive, to appear to be in the cup when there is no wine in the cup by which Christ's blood is presented so that it may be proclaimed according to the holy teaching and witness of all the scriptures. In Genesis [Gen. 9: 21–3] we find an anticipation of it and a figure of the Lord's passion in the holy teaching about Noah; he drank wine, became drunk, was made naked in his own house, and lay down with his bare legs wide open until his father's nakedness was noticed by the middle son and covered up by the eldest and the youngest, and so on. There is no need to continue, because it is sufficient to grasp the fact that Noah, presenting a type of the truth to come, drank not water but wine and thus produced a representation of the Lord's passion. And again we see the sacrament of our Lord's sacrifice prefigured in the priest Melchizedek, as attested by holy scripture in the words, "And Melchizedek king of Salem brought out bread and wine. He was the priest of God most high, and blessed Abraham" [Gen. 14: 18–20]. That Melchizedek contained a prefiguration of Christ is made plain by the Holy Spirit in one of the Psalms, where he says, in the mouth of the father speaking to his son, "I created you before

Lucifer. You are a priest for ever according to the order of Melchizedek" ' [Ps. 109: 3–4 (110: 3–4)]. This passage, like what follows in this letter, keeps to the confines of the restrained style, as readers may easily discover.

Saint Ambrose too, although treating the important subject 127 of the Holy Spirit, uses the restrained style to demonstrate his equality to the Father and the Son, because his chosen topic does not require verbal ornament or emotional fervour to move the mind, but factual evidence. So he says at the beginning of this work [Ambr. *De Spiritu* prol. 2–3], among other things, 'Gideon was persuaded by this divine pronouncement; on hearing that in the absence of thousands of fighting men the Lord would rescue his people from their enemy through one man, he offered a kid from his herds, and in accordance with the angel's instructions placed its flesh together with unleav- ened cakes on a rock and marinaded them in broth. When the angel of the Lord touched this offering with the tip of the rod that he was carrying, fire blazed out from the rock, consuming the sacrifice that was being offered [Judg. 6: 11–21]. This evi- dence seems to make it clear that the rock presents a type of Christ's body, because it is written, "They drank from the rock that followed them, and the rock was Christ" [1 Cor. 10: 4]. This surely relates not to his divinity, but to his flesh, which has refreshed the hearts of his thirsting people with the unfail- ing stream of his blood. So in this mystery it was declared even then that the crucified Lord Jesus would in his own flesh remove the sins of the whole world, and not only the sins of action, but the lusts of the heart as well. The flesh of the kid refers to the sins of action, and the broth to the seductiveness of desire, as shown by the scripture that says, "The people con- ceived a wicked desire, and said, 'who will give us flesh to eat?' " [Num. 11: 4]. The fact that the angel put out his rod and touched the rock from which the fire came shows that the Lord's flesh, filled with the Holy Spirit, would burn away all the sins of our human condition. This is why the Lord said, "I have come to put fire on the earth" ' [Luke 12: 49]. And so Ambrose goes on, intent on teaching and confirming this truth.

An example of the mixed style is Cyprian's encomium of 128 virginity [Cypr. *De Habitu Virginum* 3]. 'Now my address is

directed to virgins, whose sense of responsibility must match
their exalted reputation. This is the flower of the church's garden, the showpiece and ornament of spiritual grace, the joyous
crown of praise and honour; a creation perfect and uncor-
rupted, an image of God which reflects the Lord's holiness, a
distinguished portion of Christ's flock. In them the glorious
fecundity of their mother the church rejoices, and through
them she blossoms abundantly; and the more daughters that
prolific virginity adds to its numbers, the more the mother's joy
increases.' And in another passage, at the end of the letter, he
says [ibid. 23–4]: 'Just as we have borne the image of the earthly
man, so let us bear the image of the heavenly man [1 Cor. 15: 49].
This image is borne by virginity; it is borne by incorruptibility; it is borne by holiness and truthfulness; it is borne by
those who remember God's training, and by those who
maintain justice together with religion, by those who are firm
in their religious faith, humble in their godly fear, strong
enough for all kinds of endurance, gentle enough to put up
with injustice, always ready for acts of mercy, and united and
harmonious in brotherly peace. Noble virgins, each of you
must practise, respect, and achieve these various things; for
you, being free for God and Christ, go before us in a position of
greater and higher status towards the master to whom you have
dedicated yourselves. Those of you who are advanced in age
should give teaching to the younger ones; those who are
younger should provide a challenge to your comrades. Stimu-
late each other with mutual exhortation, challenge each other
to glory with competitive demonstrations of virtue; hold fast
with courage, proceed with the spirit, and reach your goal with
joy; only be mindful of us, when virginity begins to receive
acclaim through you.'

129   Ambrose also uses the mixed and ornate style of speaking
when, in the form of a description, he offers dedicated virgins
a standard of behaviour. He says [Ambr. *De Virginitate* 2. 2.
7–8], 'She was a virgin not only physically but also mentally,
and not the sort to taint her honest character with any attempt
to deceive; she was lowly in heart, serious in speech, prudent in
mind; an infrequent speaker, but a diligent reader; she based
her hopes not on uncertain riches [1 Tim. 6: 17] but on her

pauper's prayers; she was devoted to her work, modest in her conversation; she looked to God, not man, as the judge of her heart; she offended nobody to their face* and wished everybody well; she stood up out of respect for older people, and felt no envy towards those of her own age; she avoided ostentation, followed reason, and loved virtue. When did she offend her parents, even by her expression? When did she disagree with her relatives? When did she despise the humble? When did she mock the disabled? When did she avoid a beggar? She was careful to visit only those groups of men in which her compassionate soul would not be embarrassed that her modesty might oblige her to pass anyone by. There was no aggression in her eyes, no insolence in her words, no immodesty in her actions; her gestures were not affected; her gait was not unbecoming; her conversation was not assertive. Her whole outward appearance was a mirror of her mind and a picture of honesty. A good home should be recognized as such even in its vestibule, and should proclaim right at the entrance, as it were by light radiating from a lamp inside, that no darkness lurks within. Why should I describe her frugality in eating, and her extravagance in well-doing, the one exceeding, the other barely meeting, the requirements of nature? For the one, no opportunities were let slip; for the other, two or more whole days at a time were spent in fasting, and when she did experience a desire for refreshment it was generally for food to stave off death, not to provide enjoyment.' And so on. I have presented these two passages as examples of the mixed style, because the aim is not to make virgins of women who have not yet professed virginity, but to show women who have professed virginity how they should behave. In order to embark upon such a great undertaking, the mind must be excited and inspired by the grand style of speaking. But Cyprian the martyr was writing about the life-style of virgins, not about making a profession of virginity, whereas Ambrose the bishop was also using his great eloquence to inspire them to virginity.

I shall take my examples of the grand style from an area that they both treated. Both denounced women who colour, or rather discolour, their bodies with cosmetics. The first of them says in this regard, among other things [Cypr. *De Habitu*

Virginum 15–16]: 'Suppose an artist had depicted somebody's face, general appearance, and physical characteristics in life-like colours, and that when the painting was completely finished another artist put his hand to it, thinking himself a better painter and intending to redo what was already a finished painting: this would appear a great injustice to the first artist, and a just cause for indignation. So do you think you will get away with the insolence of your wicked effrontery and your implied insult to God the creator? Even if you are not regarded among men as indecent and revolting with your garish make-up, your corruption and violation of what is God's handiwork marks you down as worse than an adulteress. What you think of as adornment, what you think of as fashion, is an attack on God's creation, an offence against truth. This is the apostle Paul's warning [1 Cor. 5: 7–8]: "Purge out the old leaven, so that you may be a fresh mixture, unleavened just as you are. For Christ our Passover is sacrificed for us. So let us celebrate the feast, not with the old leaven or with the leaven of corruption and wickedness, but with the unleavened bread of simplicity and truth." Can simplicity and truth survive when simple things are polluted and true colours changed into false ones by artificially coloured cosmetic dyes? Your Lord says: "You cannot make a single hair black or white" [Matt. 5: 36], yet you would like to be more powerful and overthrow the words of your Lord! Staining your hair is a piece of reckless audacity and blasphemous contempt; experimenting with orange tints in your hair is an omen of hell-fire.' It would take a long time to add all that follows.

132   What the second of these writers says against such women is this [Ambr. *De Virginitate* 1. 6. 28]: 'This is the origin of these incitements to vice: the fact that they decorate their faces with artificial colours for fear of not pleasing their husbands, and that by corrupting their faces they bring about the corruption of their chastity. What great madness it is to change their natural appearance and look for an artificial one, and to betray their own judgement of themselves for fear of their husbands' judgement! The woman who wishes to change her nature makes a prior judgement on herself. And so in her eagerness to please another man, she begins by not pleasing herself. Do we

need a better judge of your ugliness than your own self, woman, something which you are afraid to show in public? If you are beautiful, why hide it? If you are ugly, why pretend you are beautiful, thus forfeiting both the benefit of your own conscience and the benefit of another person's delusion? For he loves a different woman, and you seek to please a different man; yet you would be angry if he loved another woman, even though it is by you that he is taught to be a kind of two-timer. Sadly, you are the initiator of this injustice to yourself. Even a woman exploited by a pimp shuns these allurements, and worthless as she is at least sins only against herself, and not anyone else. Sins committed in adultery are almost more tolerable; they pollute one's chastity, but not one's nature.' It is   133 clear enough, I think, that women are being strongly urged by this rhetoric not to contaminate their bodies with cosmetics, and moved to shame and fear. Accordingly we recognize in this neither the restrained nor the mixed style, but, beyond all doubt, the grand style. Both in these two writers, whom I have selected from the whole range, and in the other Christian writers who say good things and say them well—by which I mean clearly, ornately, and passionately, as the situation demands—these three styles may be found throughout their many writings or sermons; and they may be cultivated by keen students through constant reading or listening, combined with regular practice.

Nobody should think that it is against the rules of the art to   134 combine these styles. On the contrary, our discourse should be varied by using all three, as far as is possible without impropriety. When a speech carries on in a single style, it is less absorbing for the listener, but when there is transition from one style to another it has a smoother flow, even if it is rather long. It is true, however, that in the mouths of eloquent speakers the individual styles have their own kinds of variety, which prevent them from falling flat or becoming tedious to their audience. Be that as it may, the restrained style on its own is easier to tolerate over a long period than the grand style on its own. The more important it is to arouse emotion to win our   135 listener's assent, the less easy it is to sustain it for a long time once it has been sufficiently aroused. So we must take care that

in seeking to intensify what is already intense our style of speaking does not fall from the level that we reached with our emotive words. It is a good idea to introduce things that have to be said in the restrained style and then return to the things that require the grand style, so that the intensity of our speech ebbs and flows like the tides of the sea. It follows that, if we must speak for a long time, the grand style should not be used alone but be varied by the introduction of the other styles. (The discourse as a whole is assigned to the style which is preponderant
136 in terms of quantity.) It is important to know which of these styles may be combined, and which ones are applicable to particular contexts. Within the grand style an introduction should always—or almost always—be in the mixed style, and it is open to the eloquent speaker to say some things in the restrained style, even if the grand style is a possibility, so that what is said in the grand style gains prominence in comparison with them and is made to appear brighter because the rest is as it were in shadow. When, in whatever style, there are complex problems to unravel, incisiveness is required, and this is the
137 proper concern of the restrained style. Accordingly we must also use that style within the other two styles when such things crop up. Similarly, when there is something to be praised or censured but where a person's condemnation or acquittal, or an audience's assent and action, are not at issue, whatever the style in which this need arises, the mixed style must be used and introduced. So in the grand style the two other styles find their place; and in the restrained style, likewise, the other two
138 find theirs. The mixed style sometimes, but not always, requires the restrained style; when, for example, as I have just said, a question arises in which there are difficulties to be unravelled, or when topics which could have been embellished are deliberately not embellished but put in the restrained style in order to give greater prominence to particular clusters of ornament.* But a discourse in the middle style has no need of the grand style: it is employed to delight people's minds, not move them to action.
139   A speaker should not be thought to be speaking in the grand style just because he is frequently and warmly applauded; this effect is also produced by the incisiveness of the restrained

style and the embellishment of the mixed style. As a rule the grand style silences people's voices with its weight, but elicits tears. I was once appealing to the people in Caesarea of Mauretania* to abandon their civil strife, or rather that conflict worse than civil strife* which they called *caterva*, in which regularly at a particular time of the year not merely citizens, but even close relatives, brothers, and even parents and sons used to split into opposing gangs and fight with stones continuously for several days, slaughtering whomever they could. I spoke, to the best of my ability, in the grand style, in order to eradicate and eliminate such a cruel and chronic evil from their hearts and their habits by my words. I did not think I had achieved anything when I heard them applaud, but only when I saw them in tears. Their applause showed that they were receiving 140 instruction and experiencing delight; their tears that they were moved. It was when I saw this—and before they showed it in their actions—that I believed that this brutal practice, inherited from their fathers and grandfathers and remoter ancestors, which so fatally obsessed, or rather possessed, their hearts, had been overcome. Quickly finishing my speech, I occupied their hearts and mouths in giving thanks to God. And indeed through Christ's mercy it is now some eight years, or more, since such violence has been attempted. There are many other experiences by which I have learnt that people show the effects of a wise speech delivered in the grand style not by shouting so much as groaning, and sometimes even by weeping, and, eventually, by changing their lives. Many 141 people are transformed by the restrained style of speaking too, but in the sense of knowing what they did not know before or believing what had once seemed incredible to them, and not in the sense of doing something which they had known to be necessary but refused to do. To move that kind of hard-heartedness one must speak in the grand style. In the mixed style speeches of praise or blame, when given eloquently, move some people not only to a delight in the eloquent expression of praise or blame but also to a decision to live a praiseworthy life and avoid a blameworthy one; but it can hardly be said that all people who delight in such things remodel their lives, in the same way that all those who are moved by a speech in the grand style act on it, or in the same way that all who are instructed in the restrained style come to understand something or, if they do not understand it, at least believe it to be true.

142   From this it may be inferred that the aims of these two styles are a particularly important consideration for those who wish to speak eloquently and wisely. The aim of the mixed style—to give delight through the eloquence itself—should not be espoused for its own sake but so that assent for things which are spoken of for the general good and with honourable intent (assuming that the listeners know the topic and are sympathetic, and so do not require a style that instructs or moves) may as a result of this delight be gained more readily and

143   implant itself more firmly. The general function of eloquence, in any of these three styles, is to speak in a manner fitted to persuade, and the aim is to persuade people, by speaking, of what you are trying to put over; so in any of these three styles the eloquent speaker speaks in a manner fitted to persuade, and if he fails to persuade he has not achieved the aim of his eloquence. In the restrained style he persuades people that what he says is true; in the grand style he persuades them to do what they knew to be necessary but were not doing; in the mixed style he persuades people that he is speaking attractively or elaborately.

144   But what is the point of that? Let that be the aim of those who revel in verbiage, and let them show off in panegyrics and speeches of that sort, where the audience does not need to be instructed or moved to action, but merely delighted. We should relate this aim to another aim, that of achieving in this mixed style what we want to achieve in the grand style (that is, to make people love good behaviour and avoid the bad); but not if our listeners are so far from doing this that it seems necessary to urge them to it in the grand style, or if they are already doing it but need to be persuaded to do it with greater commitment and resolution. It follows that we should use the embellishment of the middle style thoughtfully, and not ostentatiously, not content with its aim of simply delighting an audience but rather intent to ensure that it helps them towards the good action which is the object of our persuasion.

145   The three aims which I stipulated earlier—when saying that the wise speaker who also wants to speak eloquently must make

it his aim to be listened to with understanding, with pleasure, and with obedience—should not be understood in the sense that a single aim is assigned to each style (so that to be listened to with understanding would be the business of the restrained style, to be listened to with pleasure that of the mixed style, and to be listened to with obedience that of the grand style), but rather in the sense that a speaker should always have these three aims and pursue them to the best of his ability even when operating within one particular style. After all, we do not want what we say in a restrained style to be despised, and so we want to be listened to not only with understanding but also with pleasure. And when we teach what we have to say with the help 146 of the divine testimonies, what is our aim if not to be listened to with obedience, or in other words, to induce belief in them, with the help of the one to whom it was said, 'your testimonies have been made very believable' [Ps. 92: 5 (93: 5)]? What is the purpose of the speaker who expounds something to his audience, even in the restrained style, if not to be believed? And who would wish to listen to him unless captivated by a certain amount of charm? Who does not realize that a person who is not understood cannot be listened to either with pleasure or with obedience? It often happens that a discourse in the 147 restrained style, as it solves very difficult problems and explains things by means of startling proofs, or uncovers and reveals some very penetrating ideas from an unexpected source (rather like treasure from a cave),* or refutes the error of our adversary and teaches that something apparently irrefutable said by him is false—especially when this is accompanied by a charm which is not contrived but somehow natural, and by a rhythm of clausulae which is not pretentious but seemingly inevitable, and arises as it were from the actual subject-matter—elicits such cheers of approval that it is not easily recognized as the restrained style. Just because it marches to battle without embellishment or 148 armour, and apparently defenceless, this does not prevent it from crushing the enemy with the strength of its sinewy hands and disabling its opponent and demolishing falsehood with its mighty limbs. How can one explain the frequent and lengthy applause given to such speakers except by the delight produced by the demonstration, the defence, and the indestructibility of the truth? So in this restrained style too our teacher and speaker must aim to be listened to not only with understanding but also with pleasure and with obedience.

149 Again, in the mouth of the Christian speaker the eloquence of the mixed style is not left without embellishment or embellished inappropriately. The aim is not only to give delight (though others make this their sole aim) but to be listened to with obedience on the matters which it subjects to praise or blame, so that the former may be sought or more resolutely followed, and the latter avoided or repudiated. But if it is not listened to with understanding it cannot be listened to with pleasure. So these three aims—that the audience understand, delight, and obey—must be sought in this style too, where

150 delight is paramount. When one needs to move and sway one's listeners—this is necessary at the point when they acknowledge that a speech is both true and delightful but are unwilling to do what it recommends—one must certainly speak in the grand style. But who can be moved if he does not understand what is said? Or who can be engrossed and made to listen, if he is not delighted? So in this style too, when hard hearts must be moved by grandeur of style, a speaker cannot be listened to with obedience unless he is also listened to with understanding and pleasure as well.

151 More important than any amount of grandeur of style to those of us who seek to be listened to with obedience is the life of the speaker. A wise and eloquent speaker who lives a wicked life certainly educates many who are eager to learn, although he is useless to his own soul, as scripture puts it [cf. Ecclus. 37: 2]. That is why Paul says, 'Let Christ be proclaimed, whether in pretence or in truth' [Phil. 1: 18]. Christ is the truth, and yet the truth can be proclaimed even by untruth, in the sense that things which are right and true may be proclaimed by a wicked and deceitful heart. It is in this way that Jesus Christ is proclaimed by those who seek their own and not the things of Jesus

152 Christ [Phil. 2: 21]. But because good, faithful men listen with obedience not to a particular speaker, but to their Lord, who says, 'Do what they say, but do not do what they do; for they do not practise what they preach' [Matt. 23: 3], even those that

behave unprofitably are heard with profit. For they may seek
their own thing, but they dare not teach their own words from
the elevated position of the episcopal chair, which sound
teaching has established. This is why the Lord himself, before
speaking the above-mentioned words on this matter, warned,
'They sit in Moses' seat' [Matt. 23: 2]. It was that seat, not
theirs but Moses', that compelled them to say good things,
even though they did not do good things. So in their own lives
they did their own thing, but in another's seat they were not
allowed to teach their own things. So they benefit many people   153
by preaching what they do not practise, but they would benefit
far more people if they practised what they preached. There
are plenty of people who look for a justification of their own
evil lives from those in authority who teach them; they reply
within their hearts or even, if they blurt it out, with their lips,
'Why don't you practise what you preach?' That is why people
do not listen with obedience to the man who does not listen to
himself, and they despise the word of God preached to them as
well as despising the preacher. Finally, the apostle Paul,   154
writing to Timothy [1 Tim. 4: 12], after saying, 'Let nobody
despise your youth', added the reason why he should not be
despised, and said, 'be an example to believers in speech, in
conduct, in love, in faith, and in purity'. For such a teacher,   155
seeking to be listened to with obedience, it is not impudent to
speak not only in the restrained and the mixed styles but also in
the grand style, because the life he lives is not a contemptible
one. He has chosen to live a good life without neglecting a good
reputation; and to the best of his ability he aims at what is
honourable in the eyes of God and man [2 Cor. 8: 21], by fear-
ing the one and taking thought for the other. When actually
speaking he should choose to satisfy his audience with things
rather than words, and not regard any matter as better
expressed than another unless it is more truthfully expressed;
the words must serve the teacher, not the other way round.
This is what the apostle Paul meant when he said, 'not with the
wisdom of words, lest the cross of Christ be emptied of power'
[1 Cor. 1: 17]. What he said to Timothy is also important: 'do   156
not do battle with words; this is useless, and only ruins those
who listen' [2 Tim. 2: 14]. But this was not said to deter us from

saying anything in defence of the truth when our enemies
attack it. Otherwise what would be the point of saying, as he
did say (among other things), to show what kind of person a
bishop should be, 'so that he may be strong in sound teaching
and able to refute those who oppose it'? [Titus 1: 9]. To 'do
battle with words' is to be concerned not about overcoming
error with truth, but about making your sermon seem better
157 than someone else's. The speaker who avoids battles over
words is the one who endeavours in his words, whether speaking in the restrained, the mixed, or the grand style, to make the
truth clear, to make it pleasing, and to make it moving, since
not even the love which is the end of the commandment and
the fulfilment of the law [cf. 1 Tim. 1: 5, Rom. 13: 10] can be
directed aright if the things loved are not true but false. Just as
a person who has a handsome body but a repulsive mind is
more pathetic than if he had a repulsive body as well, so those
who speak eloquently of what is false are more to be pitied than
158 if they spoke of it repulsively. Surely, then, the art of speaking
both eloquently and wisely is a matter of using adequate words
in the restrained style, striking words in the mixed style, and
powerful words in the grand style, but using them of things
that are true and need to be heard. But the speaker who cannot
do both should treat wisely what he cannot treat eloquently
159 rather than the reverse. If he is not even capable of this, he
should seek to live in such a way that he not only gains a reward
for himself but also gives an example to others, so that his way
of life becomes, in a sense, an abundant source of eloquence.

160   There are indeed some people who can give a good speech
but not compose one. If they borrow from others something
composed with eloquence and wisdom and commit it to
memory and then bring that to their audience, they are not
doing anything wrong, provided that they adhere to this role.
Moreover it is in this way—and this is certainly a useful
thing—that many men become preachers of the truth, but few
are teachers of it, provided that they all really speak the words
of the one true teacher 'and there are no divisions among them'
[1 Cor. 1: 10]. They should not be inhibited by the words of the
prophet Jeremiah, through whom God condemns those who
161 'steal words, each one from his neighbour' [Jer. 23: 30]. People

who steal take something that is not their own, but it is not the case that the word of God is not theirs, if they obey him. It is rather those who speak well but live evil lives that speak something that is not their own. The good things they say seem to be the product of their own brains, but are at odds with their behaviour. Those who, as God said, steal his words are those who want to appear good by saying the things of God when in fact they are evil, doing their own thing. But if you think carefully, it is not they themselves that speak the good things they say. For how can they affirm in their words what they deny in their actions? The apostle Paul had a point when he said about such people: 'They profess to know God, but deny him in their actions' [Titus 1: 16]. In one sense it is they themselves who speak, but in another sense it is not they themselves who speak: both these things are true, as the truth says. On the one hand, 162 when speaking about such men, Christ says 'do what they say but not what they do' [Matt. 23: 3] (that is, 'do what you hear from their mouths but not what you see in their actions'), for 'they do not practise what they preach'. They do at least preach, even if they do not practise. But in another passage he rebukes such people: 'Hypocrites, how can you say good things, when you are evil?' [Matt. 12: 34]. It follows that when they say good things it is not they themselves who say them, because in their wills and actions they deny what they say. So it 163 is possible for a person who is eloquent but evil actually to compose a sermon proclaiming the truth for another, who is not eloquent but good, to deliver. When this happens, one person transfers from himself what is not his own, and one receives from the other what is his own. But when good and faithful people lend such a work to others who are good and faithful, both parties are saying what is their own, because the God to whom their words belong is their own, and because people who live aright, according to what they have been unable to write for themselves, make such writings their own. Whether they are going to speak before a congregation or any 164 other body, or to dictate something to be spoken before a congregation or read by others who are able and willing to do so, speakers must pray that God will place a good sermon on their lips. If Queen Esther, when about to plead before the king

for the temporal salvation of her people, prayed that God
would place a suitable speech on her lips [Esth. 14: 13], how
much more important is it for those who work for people's
eternal salvation 'by teaching God's word' [1 Tim. 5: 17] to
165 pray to receive such a gift? Those who are going to deliver
something they have received from others should pray, before
receiving it, that those from whom they will get it may be given
what they, through them, want to receive. They should also
pray, after receiving it, that they themselves may present it
effectively and that those to whom they present it may absorb
it effectively. And they should also give thanks for a favourable
outcome of their address to the one from whom they do not
doubt that they received it, 'so that anyone who boasts may
boast' in the one 'whose hands hold us and our sermons alike'
[1 Cor. 1: 31; Wisd. 7: 16].

166   This book has ended up longer than I wanted or expected it
to be; but it is not too long for the reader or hearer who wel-
comes it. Anybody who finds it too long should read it in parts
if he wants to have a complete knowledge of it, and anybody
who is not interested in such knowledge should not complain
of its length. But in any case I thank God that in these four
books I have been able to discuss, with such ability as I have,
not the sort of person that I am—for I have many failings—but
the sort of person that those who apply themselves to sound
teaching [Titus 1: 9], in other words Christian teaching, on
behalf of others as well as themselves, ought to be.

Explanatory Notes

Adv. Haer.	*Adversus Haereses*
Ambr.	Ambrose
Conf.	*Confessiones*
Cypr.	Cyprian
DDC	*De Doctrina Christiana*
De Div. Quaest.	*De Diversis Quaestionibus lxxxiii*
Demonstr.	*Demonstratio*
De Trin.	*De Trinitate*
Enarr.	*Enarrationes*
Enarr. in Ps.	*Enarrationes in Psalmos*
Enn.	*Enneads*
Ep.	*Epistula*
In Ps.	*In Psalmos*
JTS	*Journal of Theological Studies*
PG	*Patrologia Graeca*
REA	*Revue des Études Augustiniennes*
Rech. Aug.	*Recherches Augustiniennes*
Retract.	*Retractationes*
Rhet. Her.	*Rhetorica ad Herennium*
Serm.	*Sermones*
Tract. Ioh.	*Tractatus in Iohannem*
TU	*Texte und Untersuchungen*
VC	*Vigiliae Christianae*

3 *themselves*: illumination to benefit themselves and others; the former goal is uppermost in Books 1–3, the latter dominates Book 4.

A third class of critic: Augustine probably has in mind not a particular group (as suggested by U. Duchrow in 'Zum Prolog von Augustins *De Doctrina Christiana*', *VC* 17 (1963), 165–72), but a more general tendency to 'charismatic' interpretation.

4 *Anthony*: *The Life of Anthony*, by Athanasius, emphasizes Anthony's lifelong lack of letters (1. 72–3), but has nothing to say about his learning of the scriptures.

Christian slave: nothing more is known of this man.

I ask you!: here Augustine has adapted a phrase commonly used to protest at something outrageous.

5 *faith, hope, and love*: as described in Acts 10. The words on faith, hope, and love are Augustine's addition.

6 *except perhaps a lie*: this is derived from John 8: 44, which in Augustine's text had the sense 'he who speaks a lie speaks of his own'.

8 *discovery*: 'discovery' (Latin *inventio*) is a technical term of classical rhetoric, defined by one authority as 'the devising of plausible matter to make a case convincing' (*Rhet. Her.* 1. 2. 3). It will be obvious that Augustine, who aims to enable readers to discover in scripture basic truths about God and encouragements to the double love of God and one's neighbour, has significantly changed its meaning.

great and arduous burden: an adaptation of a phrase of Cicero (*Orator* 33), which he quotes verbatim at the beginning of *City of God*.

9 *consists in signifying*: see 2. 1–8.

estranged: or 'alienated'; for this notion, and a discussion of possible sources, see R. A. Markus, '*Alienatio*: Philosophy and Eschatology in the Development of an Augustinian Idea', *TU* 94 (1966), 431–50.

10 *conflict between words here*: in *Enn.* 5. 3. 14 Plotinus discusses this point, in relation to the absolute One (the supreme being in his philosophy), and concludes that although it is unspeakable we may speak about it and say what it is not.

11 *two syllables*: Latin *deus* ('god') has two syllables.

those who are devoted to the bodily senses: this category takes in the pre-Socratic philosophers, Plato, Aristotle, Stoics, and Epicureans, as well as popular belief.

through their intellect: especially the Neoplatonists (cf. 2. 144). Their concepts are prominent in the following paragraphs, in which Augustine draws frequently on Plotinus.

12 *wisdom itself*: the process just described matches Augustine's 'ascent', as he describes it in *Conf.* 7. 17. 23.

and never can be: in *Enn.* 5. 9. 2 Plotinus differentiates 'the true Intellect' (roughly, the divine mind) from a human intellect in the same way—it is not 'sometimes intellect and sometimes unintelligent'.

standard of truth: Plotinus uses this concept in *Enn.* 1. 3. 5, when discussing how dialectic (logic) enables one to recognize falsehood. Augustine may have taken the idea from him, but does not specify how exactly it should be conceived in the present context.

purified: purification is an important concept in Plotinus. In *Enn.* 3. 6. 5 he asks whether the purification of the soul is the same as separation from the body (discussing Plato *Phaedo* 67c), and in

1. 6. 9 he talks of the need for an eye not blurred by wickedness or weakened by cowardice (compare Augustine at 1. 24).

13 *a trek, or a voyage, to our homeland*: the same metaphor of travel is found in Plotinus, *Enn.* 1. 6. 8, a vivid passage which impressed Augustine. 'Our country from which we came is there, our Father is there. How shall we travel to it . . .? We cannot get there on foot . . . You must not get ready a carriage, either, or a boat.' Echoes of this are present in the following chapters, and in *Confessions*.

14 *suffering no diminution from its change*: this point is based on Wisd. 7: 27. On the relation of words and Word, see especially *De Trin.* 15. 14. 23–16. 26.

16 *or both*: the following analysis of love in terms of 'use' and 'enjoyment' is something unique to this work of Augustine; for a detailed study see O. O'Donovan, '*Usus* and *Fruitio* in Augustine *De Doctrina Christiana* I', *JTS* NS 33 (1982), 361–97.

19 *inferior*: cf. *Conf.* 7. 17. 23, where Augustine speaks of repeatedly 'crashing into inferior things', through the weight of sexual habits.

perverse contracts: a favourite and important notion of Augustine, used rather differently in 2. 74–95. Cf. also *Conf.* 1. 18. 29, where he contrasts his teachers' high valuation of the conventions of spelling with their neglect of the God-given contracts of lasting salvation.

21 *ordered his love*: on the notion of 'ordering' one's love see O. O'Donovan, *The Problem of Self-Love in St. Augustine* (New Haven, 1980), 24–32.

should be loved more: the words included in brackets have been added to complete the sense; the absence from all manuscripts of their Latin counterparts is surely accidental.

22 *den of wickedness*: a common complaint of Augustine; cf. 2. 71. He is thinking not of plays but of various kinds of popular entertainment such as sexually explicit mimes.

25 *in the Lord*: a rather unusual way of describing love, found again in 3. 37. Cf. also *Ep.* 26. 4.

26 *transferred sense*: what Augustine means by this 'transferred' sense is clear in 3. 89, where he speaks of the figure of *abusio* or catachresis.

27 *wants to be misled*: there is a fuller treatment of this and other questions about lying in Augustine's treatises *De Mendacio* and *Contra Mendacium*.

30 *I began with the warning . . . might signify*: 1. 4.

that they signify: there are illuminating analyses of Augustine's

theory of signs by R. A. Markus in 'St. Augustine on Signs', *Phrone-
sis*, 2 (1957), 60–83, and B. D. Jackson in 'The Theory of Signs in
St. Augustine's *De Doctrina Christiana*', *REA* 15 (1969), 9–49—
both reprinted in R. A. Markus (ed.), *Collected Essays on Augustine*
(New York, 1972), 61–91, 92–147—and in C. Kirwan, *Augustine*
(London, 1989), 35–43.

32 *a single language*: Hebrew for the Old Testament, Greek for the
New.

I have no doubt … reinvigorated: Augustine makes similar statements
in 4. 27, *Ep*. 55. 11. 21, and *Ep*. 137. 18. See also J. Pepin, 'Saint
Augustin et la fonction protreptique de l'allégorie', in *Rech. Aug*. 1
(1958), 244–57.

love of God and love of their neighbour: the same interpretation of the
two lambs is found in *Ep*. 149. 1. 4 and *Serm*. 313B. 3.

33 *fear of God*: the following description of the seven steps or stages to
wisdom is closely based on the description of the gifts of the spirit
found (in the reverse order) in Isa. 11: 2–3.

34 *resolve of compassion*: Latin versions of Isaiah (11: 2–3) give *consilium*
('resolve'), with no mention of compassion; hence Augustine's
strained expression.

36 *canon of scripture*: the details of this canon, and its relationship to
other contemporary African versions, is discussed by A.-M. Bonnardière, 'Le Canon des divines Écritures', in A.-M. Bonnardière
(ed.), *Saint Augustin et la Bible*, iii (Paris, 1986), 287–301.

the two of Ezra: Ezra and Nehemiah.

Jesus Sirach wrote them: Augustine withdrew this statement in
Retract. 2. 30. 2, after he had realized that in all probability Jesus
Sirach was not their author. See also Bonnardière, *Saint Augustin et
la Bible*, iii. 294–8.

37 *Colossians*: Colossians was usually placed after Thessalonians in the
early Western church.

previous book: see especially 1. 90–6.

38 *passage in Isaiah*: the first reading given is that of the Septuagint, the
second a more literal translation used in the Vulgate.

39 *again from Isaiah*: the readings quoted are those of the Septuagint
and Symmachus respectively. Augustine has the second in *De Trin*.
7. 6 and 15. 2.

40 *hard to find*: in fact no extant witnesses agree with Augustine.

solecism: a solecism occurs if the concord (or grammatical agreement) between two words in the same group is faulty ('the vegetables was cold'), a barbarism if a verbal expression is incorrect (especially if it comes from an unsuitable register or the speech of a different race: so 'spud' or 'tattie' for 'potato'). These definitions (but not the examples) are based on the classical definitions in *Rhet. Her.* 4. 12. 17 and Quintilian 1. 5.

hominibus: the meaning is the same ('among men'), but only the first is good Latin.

ignoscere: 'to forgive'. In what follows Augustine means 'vowel', not 'syllable'.

41 *what is the land . . . live in them?*: in the Septuagint version, which follows Hebrew idiom closely.

the Greek expression: this would mean using the genitive case to express comparison, which it does not do in classical Latin.

huic homini or hoc homine: the former is in the dative case, the latter in the ablative.

42 *the Itala*: an Italian version of the pre-Vulgate text; further identification with extant witnesses has proved impossible.

Its seventy writers . . . a single voice: on this and other details see S. Jellicoe, *The Septuagint and Modern Study* (Oxford, 1968), 29–58.

43 *King Ptolemy*: Ptolemy Philadelphus (285–246 BC), as stated in Augustine's longer account in *City of God* 18. 42.

above: cf. 2. 43.

44 *Various experts . . . the scriptures*: notably Jerome, in his *Liber Interpretationis Hebraicorum Nominum* and *Liber Locorum*, a gazetteer based on a work of Eusebius. For further details see J. N. D. Kelly, *Jerome* (London, 1975), 153–5.

which means that . . . deny God: this interpretation is the usual one in the Latin fathers of that time.

is said to take on new strength: for example, by Servius in his commentary on Virgil *Aeneid* 2. 473.

hyssop: cf. 2. 150.

45 *the four elements . . . obvious*: air, fire, earth, and water.

Pentecost: Pentecost means literally 'fiftieth' (day).

46 *there are some figurative meanings . . . the lyre*: the author of this insight, often exploited in Augustine's *Enarrationes in Psalmos*, is not known.

the Son of God . . . insubstantial one: there is further discussion of this point by Augustine in *Tract. Ioh.* 10. 10–12, *De Div. Quaest.* 56, *De Trin.* 4. 5.

46 *Varro*: the Roman polymath of the first century BC, praised no less highly in *City of God* 6. 2. The present point was probably made in one or both of his lost works *Antiquitates* and *De Musica*.

its name: not known; perhaps Helicon in Boeotia.

47 *gave them names*: Hesiod *Theogony* 50–5.

threefold: Augustine's contemporary Ausonius gives a different threefold division—celestial, human, and orchestral music—in 15. 77.

We were not wrong . . . patron: a point conceded even by the rigorist Tertullian (*De Corona* 8. 2).

48 *contracts*: explained in sections 87–95.

poets: the Roman writers of epic Virgil (*Aeneid* 4. 478–98) and Lucan (*Bellum Civile* 6. 413–830), among many others. Augustine clearly wishes to defend the poets from blame.

haruspices: soothsayers who foretold the future by inspecting the entrails of animals.

49 *Cato . . . mice*: this quip is otherwise unattested, but fits the general picture of the blunt and sceptical Cato (cf. Cicero, *De Divinatione* 2. 51). For another such mouse joke, see ibid. 2. 59.

mathematici: cf. *De Div. Quaest.* 45. 1, where Augustine notes that the term was once confined to astronomers. On Augustine's 'struggle with astrology' in general, see F. van der Meer, *Augustine the Bishop* (London, 1961), 60–7.

Caesar: probably Julius Caesar, in view of his alleged descent from Venus (claimed in Virgil's *Aeneid* and elsewhere), but corroboratory evidence for this proposal is lacking. Augustine's pseudo-legal explanation is pure burlesque.

Quinctilis and Sextilis: the original Roman names for these months, meaning 'fifth' and 'sixth' respectively. Like the modern names for the last four months of the year (closely modelled on the Roman names) they presuppose a year beginning in March.

50 *invalid*: the following argument was commonly used, and occasionally refuted, by pagan writers as well as Christian ones. Augustine uses it in several places, including *Conf.* 7. 6. 8–10 and *City of God* 5. 1–6.

It follows that . . . quite different: cf. *Conf.* 7. 6. 8–10 and *De Div. Quaest.* 45, where the same point is made.

51 *The fact that . . . King Saul*: discussed by Augustine in his contemporary *Diversae Quaestiones ad Simplicianum* 2. 3, and later in the sixth item of *Octo Dulcitii Quaestiones*.

52 *one thing . . . something else*: 'speak' and 'read' respectively. Latin *beta* is 'beet'.

54 *nothing should be thought . . . lies and falsehoods*: see note to p. 6.

some human institutions . . . natural ones: these 'natural' human institutions—the adjective is not used elsewhere in this context—are those observed by man and divinely instituted, of which discussion begins in section 104.

above: cf. 2. 50.

55 *using Olympiads and the names of consuls*: Greek reckoning was based on the period of four years between successive Olympic Games, while the Romans used the names of the two consuls in each year.

Greek scholars: notably Eusebius (cf. note to p. 64, below).

Jeremiah: Augustine later realized his mistake in claiming that Ambrose had made Plato and Jeremiah contemporaries (*Retract.* 2. 30. 2; cf. *City of God* 8. 11).

Pythagoras: the philosopher of the sixth century BC.

56 *earlier*: cf. 2. 59.

'characters': cf. 2. 75.

58 *true statements*: this passage is analysed in terms of the logic developed by the Stoic school of philosophy: see B. D. Jackson, 'The Theory of Signs in St. Augustine's *De Doctrina Christiana*', *REA* 15 (1969), 39–40.

61 *eloquence*: cf. 4. 6 for a similarly discursive definition, and Book 4 in general for a fuller treatment of the subject.

the expression of love: in technical terms, the *captatio benevolentiae* ('attempt to gain goodwill'), an important feature of an orator's prooemium.

62 *made it long*: in *Aeneid* 1. 2 and elsewhere.

63 *odd numbers are not divisible by two*: according to Augustine in *Ep.* 3. 2 odd (or 'intelligible') numbers admit of infinite increase but not infinite division.

now clever, now not: cf. note to p. 12 ('*and never can be*').

logic and number: the disciplines of definition and rhetoric (sections 129–35) are ignored.

64 *'nothing in excess'*: this ancient commonplace was given its definitive Latin form by the comic poet Terence in *Andria* 61.

Some scholars . . . interpretation: such onomastica of Hebrew and Aramaic names, and in particular those of Jerome, have been thoroughly studied by F. Wutz in 'Onomastica Sacra', *TU* 41 (1914).

Eusebius . . . chronology: for scholarly discussion of the details of Eusebius' important work, and its significance, see A. A. Mosshammer, *The Chronicle of Eusebius and Greek Chronographic Tradition* (Lewisburg, Pa., and London, 1979), 29–83 and T. D. Barnes, *Constantine and Eusebius* (Cambridge, Mass., 1981), 111–25.

jealous ones conceal them: this comment could be the result of personal disappointment; had Augustine once perhaps approached Jerome for such a work?

later: in Book 3.

Platonists: Augustine refers to the important school of philosophers now known as Neoplatonists in virtue of their extensive redevelopment of Plato: see Introduction, p. xii and H. Chadwick, *Augustine* (Oxford, 1986), 17–24.

65 *poor use*: this interpretation is also found in the third-century Greek theologian Origen (*PG* 11. 87–91), and in part resembles the figurative interpretation found in the Latin version of Irenaeus, *Adv. Haer.* 4. 46–7, which may well date from Augustine's time. The notion of 'spoiling the Egyptians' occurs also in *Conf.* 7. 9. 15. The morality of the Hebrews' action is discussed by Augustine in *De Div. Quaest.* 53, *Enarr. in Ps.* 104. 28, and *Contra Faustum* 71.

false and superstitious fantasies and burdensome studies: these aspects of pagan studies are much more evident in *Confessions* than in the preceding chapters.

Lactantius, and Victorinus, of Optatus, and Hilary: famous Christian writers of the fourth century. On Lactantius see J. Quasten, *Patrology*, 2 (1953), 392–410 and R. M. Ogilvie, *The Library of Lactantius* (Oxford, 1978), and on the others [J. Quasten] A. di Berardino (ed.), *Patrology*, 4 (Eng. trans.: Westminster, Md., 1986), 36–61, 69–80, 122–7.

people still alive: these surely include Ambrose, an important indication of the date of the work. See Introduction, pp. ix–x.

66 *to comprehend . . . height and depth*: this passage is linked with the cross by the second-century theologian Irenaeus (*Demonstr.* 34). See J. Danielou, *A History of Early Christian Doctrine*, i. *The Theology of Jewish Christianity* (London, 1964), 279–92.

67 *with his head inflated*: the Latin words used here recall a line of the
Roman satirist Persius (1. 14).

68 *emendation*: for ancient views of what was involved in 'emending' a
text, see J. E. G. Zetzel, *Latin Textual Criticism in Antiquity* (Salem,
Mass., 1981), 206–10.

Book 2: 2. 32–3.

punctuated and articulated: ancient readers often had to punctuate for
themselves: see S. F. Bonner, *Education in Ancient Rome* (London,
1977), 220–2.

the rule of faith: by this Augustine (and Aquinas after him) means the
fundamentals of Christian doctrine. On the early history of the concept, see J. N. D. Kelly, *Early Christian Creeds* (London, 1972),
76–88; on Aquinas' use of it, see J. Wawrykow, 'Reflections on the
Place of the *De doctrina christiana* in High Scholastic Discussions
of Theology', in E. D. English (ed.), *Reading and Wisdom: The De
doctrina christiana of Augustine in the Middle Ages* (Notre Dame, Ind.,
1995), 111–14.

69 *heretical punctuation*: the Arians are meant. As Augustine explains,
their revised punctuation radically changed the theological significance of the passage.

on your account: an English translation of these words cannot illustrate the ambiguity, because its word-order, unlike the Latin word-
order, determines the meaning. The point here was important in
debates with the Manichees, who saw in it evidence for the existence
of two conflicting natures in the human soul: see *Conf.* 8. 10. 23–4.

the conclusion that . . . two things: the conclusion is not inescapable;
the omission of *enim* in the Vulgate did not close the question. In fact
Augustine's first argument is the stronger one.

no one: again an English translation inevitably removes the ambiguity under discussion.

70 *ancient authorities*: such as the Roman grammarians Quintilian (9. 2. 6)
and Donatus (also the teacher of Jerome) in his commentary on
Terence *Andria* 800.

71 *But I fail to see . . . a question*: English translations do not convey this
ambiguity, and cannot, because the word-order of a question in
English differs from that of a statement; this is not the case in Latin.

Non est absconditum . . . in abscondito: literally, 'my bone/mouth,
which you made in a hidden place, is not hidden from you'.

a barbarism: cf. 2. 45 for barbarisms, and 4. 64–6 for the overriding importance of clarity. He does not champion barbarisms for their own sake, and uses them sparingly himself: see R. P. H. Green, 'Augustine's *De Doctrina Christiana*: Some Clarifications', *Respublica Litterarum*, 15 (1992), 99–108.

71 *Quae praedico . . . non possidebunt*: 'I warn you, as I have warned already, that those who do such things will not inherit the kingdom of God.'

pronounce the middle syllable . . . long or short: the former would mean 'foretell'. Again Augustine means 'vowel', not 'syllable'.

72 *in Greek . . . signifying an oath*: the problem is that Latin *per* has various meanings, unlike the Greek word used in oaths.

73 *pedagogue*: the function of a pedagogue was to see a child safely to and from school.

74 *Thou, father Neptune . . . rivers meander*: the author and context of this passage are unknown.

Anyone . . . my meaning: an allusion to Luke 15: 16, similarly used by Jerome in *Ep*. 21. 13. 4.

76 *on account of God*: cf. 1. 79.

79 *it was considered wicked . . . with sleeves*: this is derived from one of Cicero's most famous speeches, *In Catilinam* 2. 22.

justice has no absolute existence . . . as just: the reference is probably to a speaker who puts forward this thesis in Cicero's work *De Republica* (3. 9 ff.), a work from which Augustine quotes in the *City of God*.

80 *He who . . . shall lose it*: Augustine clearly takes his text to be a command, not a statement of fact.

84 *take up . . . into the understanding*: critics are aware of the faulty logic of this passage, but satisfactory explanation or emendation has not been forthcoming.

85 *leavened*: it was here that Augustine broke off, to resume some thirty years later.

87 *Could God . . . inspired passages*: this matter is dealt with more fully in the second half of *Conf*. 12.

other literature: cf. 2. 50.

88 *learning languages*: cf. 2. 43.

'allegory', 'enigma', and 'parable': cf. Gal. 4: 24 for 'allegory' and 1 Cor. 13: 12 for 'enigma'; 'parable' is much commoner.

'liberal' arts: the arts or disciplines which it was considered worth

while for a free man—or rather a man (sometimes woman) of some wealth and status—to learn. Cf. *Conf.* 4. 1. 1.

Don't we all . . . for fish: a stock example among ancient grammarians.

catachresis: this term denotes the use of a word in a context where strictly speaking it does not apply (e.g. 'substantial' for 'big', or 'menu' and 'mouse' in computer language).

lucus . . . little light: another old chestnut.

'there's plenty': compare perhaps the modern 'no problem' or (in some contexts) 'I'm delighted'.

'beware . . . a good man': it is not clear whether Augustine means that the meaning of 'beware' is coloured by 'good', and so means 'look out for', or the reverse (so that 'good' means 'bad'), which would be more truly a contrary interpretation.

all the uneducated: Quintilian pointed out (8. 6. 4) that metaphor was so natural a turn of speech that it was often employed by uneducated persons.

89 *Tyconius*: on Tyconius, an early pioneer in the area of Biblical hermeneutics, see Introduction, p. ix and H. Chadwick, 'Tyconius and Augustine', in H. Chadwick, *Heresy and Orthodoxy in the Early Church* (Aldershot, 1991), 49–55, and in general P. Monceaux, *Histoire littéraire de l'Afrique chrétienne* (Paris, 1920), v. 165–219, esp. 178–95.

The Book of Rules: see F. C. Burkitt, *The Book of Rules of Tyconius* (Cambridge, 1894), and the translation of W. S. Babcock, *Tyconius, The Book of Rules* (Atlanta, 1989).

Revelation: Tyconius' commentary on this book is lost. Augustine may have used it in his interpretation of the sixth rule, since his understanding of recapitulation differs from that of *The Book of Rules*. See M. Dulaey, 'La Sixième Règle de Tyconius et son résumé dans le *De Doctrina Christiana*', *REA* 35 (1989), 83–103.

90 *'I have thought . . . preserved from error'*: this is Tyconius' preface.

have to offer: as a rule Augustine takes one or two of Tyconius' shorter examples.

91 *an alternative title . . . on this subject*: Augustine's work of this title was written in 412.

95 *one evangelist says . . . his clothes like snow*: Matt. 17: 1–2 (six days); Mark 9: 1–2 (six); Luke 9: 28 (eight). Augustine gives the same explanation in his *De Consensu Evangelistarum* 2. 56. 113, 3. 24. 66.

101 *'There are two things . . . of presentation'*: see 1. 1.

101 *of good character*: reminiscent of Quintilian's specification of the perfect orator (12. 1. 1, from Cato), as 'a good man experienced in speaking'.

truth and falsehood: cf. 2. 132, on which this important paragraph is based.

succinct, lucid, and convincing: the virtues of the various sections of a speech, alluded to here, are succinctly given in Cicero *De Oratore* 2. 80, and in more detail at *Rhet. Her.* 1. 4. 6 ff. and Cicero *De Inventione* 1. 15. 20 ff.

102 *eloquence*: cf. 2. 132.

if these things . . . learnt at all: this point is made in Cicero *De Oratore* 3. 89, in an imagined conversation between leading orators of the generation before Cicero.

canon: cf. 2. 26–9.

the rule of holiness and faith: cf. 3. 5.

103 *They observe . . . to become eloquent*: for this point Augustine could claim the authority of the speakers in Cicero *De Oratore* 1. 87, 91.

the art of grammar: although omitted in Book 2, grammar was a vital part of the traditional curriculum: see S. F. Bonner, *Education in Ancient Rome* (London, 1977), 198–211.

divine scriptures: this and the following paragraph take up the manifesto of 4. 4, including its implied fourfold division of the speaker's task.

104 *entreaties, rebukes, rousing speeches, solemn admonitions*: the wording is similar in style and content to both Cicero *De Oratore* 3. 118 and 1 Tim. 2: 1.

they declared . . . never beneficial: Cicero *De Inventione* 1. 1. It is characteristic of Augustine to use the plural in such references to a single author.

father of lights: Augustine evidently associates the 'lights' of this phrase with the classical metaphor of *lumina dicendi* ('adornments of speech').

105 *with eloquence as well*: cf. 2. 146.

106 *The fusion . . . exertion*: cf. 2. 9.

qualities and figures of eloquence: on tropes in scripture cf. 3. 87.

107 *gradatio*: examples of this are given in *Rhet. Her.* 4. 25. 34, Quintilian 9. 3. 54–7.

Another ornament . . . the last clause: the traditional methods of analysing discourse into commata, cola, and periods are most clearly illustrated by Quintilian 9. 4. 22 and 122–30, and Augustine's contemporary Martianus Capella (5. 527–8). It is not clear how Augustine distinguishes between *membra* (limbs) and *caesa* (pieces): it is not by rhythm, length, or syntactical function.

109 *periods . . . fewer than two*: cf. Quintilian 9. 4. 125: 'the period must have at least two cola'.

110 *sold with great showmanship*: cf. 4. 144. It is also a prominent theme in *Conf.*, e.g. at 4. 2. 2 and 8. 6. 13.

111 *the translation . . . Jerome*: this is a reference to the translation we know as the Vulgate: see M. Moreau, 'Sur un commentaire d'Amos', in A.-M. Bonnardière, *Saint Augustin et la Bible*, 313–22, and A.-M. Bonnardière, 'Augustin a-t-il utilisé la Vulgate de Jérôme?', ibid. 303–12. On the Septuagint, see 2. 54 and note to p. 42.

112 *highlighted as it were*: cf. Cicero *Orator* 163, where he describes a line of verse as 'lit up with glorious place names'.

three bipartite periods: although they are not complete sentences.

114 *if the figure . . . learnt and taught*: it is not.

the things that are learnt . . . minds of orators: a point made in Cicero *De Oratore* 1. 146.

115 *'contrived casualness'*: derived from Cicero *Orator* 78, 'there is also a contrived kind of casualness' (referring to the plain or simple style of speaking).

bloods: cf. note to p. 71.

117 *he is being taught*: rather than delighted; Augustine anticipates the distinction he is about to make.

the eloquent . . . move their listeners: Cicero *Orator* 69, with a slight difference: where Augustine uses a word for 'instruct', Cicero used one meaning 'prove' or 'demonstrate'.

123 *'So the eloquent speaker . . . a grand style'*: this follows Cicero *Orator* 101, but Cicero used the word 'impressive' where Augustine uses 'grand'.

129 *the learned Jerome . . . some of them*: their metrical nature was pointed out by Jerome in his *Prologus in Iob*.

130 *'anger . . . supplies'*: Virgil *Aeneid* 7. 507–8, a vivid and (in Latin) very concise phrase which Augustine may have had to paraphrase as a school exercise.

131 *climax*: cf. note to p. 107.

135 *she offended nobody to their face*: a reminiscence of Terence *Adelphi* 864. Terence was one of the authors commonly read at school.

138 *when topics . . . clusters of ornament*: based on an insight of Cicero in *Orator* 21.

139 *I was once . . . Mauretania*: in 418. For details of this visit, see G. Bonner, 'Augustine's Visit to Caesarea in 418', in C. W. Dugmore and C. Duggan (eds.), *Studies in Church History*, 1 (London, 1964), 104–13.

conflict worse than civil strife: based on the phrase 'wars even worse than civil wars' in the first line of Lucan's epic poem *Bellum Civile*.

141 *It often happens . . . from a cave*: one of the characteristics of the plain style according to Cicero was that 'penetrating and frequent points will be made, unearthed from some unexpected sources' (*Orator* 79).

Index of Biblical Passages Cited

Index

A SELECTION OF **OXFORD WORLD'S CLASSICS**

THOMAS AQUINAS	Selected Philosophical Writings
GEORGE BERKELEY	Principles of Human Knowledge and Three Dialogues
EDMUND BURKE	A Philosophical Enquiry into the Origin of Our Ideas of the Sublime and Beautiful Reflections on the Revolution in France
THOMAS CARLYLE	The French Revolution
CONFUCIUS	The Analects
FRIEDRICH ENGELS	The Condition of the Working Class in England
JAMES GEORGE FRAZER	The Golden Bough
THOMAS HOBBES	Human Nature and De Corpore Politico Leviathan
JOHN HUME	Dialogues Concerning Natural Religion and The Natural History of Religion Selected Essays
THOMAS MALTHUS	An Essay on the Principle of Population
KARL MARX	Capital The Communist Manifesto
J. S. MILL	On Liberty and Other Essays Principles of Economy and Chapters on Socialism
FRIEDRICH NIETZSCHE	On the Genealogy of Morals Twilight of the Idols
THOMAS PAINE	Rights of Man, Common Sense, and Other Political Writings
JEAN-JACQUES ROUSSEAU	Discourse on Political Economy and The Social Contract Discourse on the Origin of Inequality
SIMA QIAN	Historical Records
ADAM SMITH	An Inquiry into the Nature and Causes of the Wealth of Nations
MARY WOLLSTONECRAFT	Political Writings

A SELECTION OF   OXFORD WORLD'S CLASSICS

JANE AUSTEN	Catharine and Other Writings
	Emma
	Mansfield Park
	Northanger Abbey, Lady Susan, The Watsons, and Sanditon
	Persuasion
	Pride and Prejudice
	Sense and Sensibility
ANNE BRONTË	Agnes Grey
	The Tenant of Wildfell Hall
CHARLOTTE BRONTË	Jane Eyre
	The Professor
	Shirley
	Villette
EMILY BRONTË	Wuthering Heights
WILKIE COLLINS	The Moonstone
	No Name
	The Woman in White
CHARLES DARWIN	The Origin of Species
CHARLES DICKENS	The Adventures of Oliver Twist
	Bleak House
	David Copperfield
	Great Expectations
	Hard Times
	Little Dorrit
	Martin Chuzzlewit
	Nicholas Nickleby
	The Old Curiosity Shop
	Our Mutual Friend
	The Pickwick Papers
	A Tale of Two Cities

GEORGE ELIOT	Adam Bede
	Daniel Deronda
	Middlemarch
	The Mill on the Floss
	Silas Marner
ELIZABETH GASKELL	Cranford
	The Life of Charlotte Brontë
	Mary Barton
	North and South
	Wives and Daughters
THOMAS HARDY	Far from the Madding Crowd
	Jude the Obscure
	The Mayor of Casterbridge
	A Pair of Blue Eyes
	The Return of the Native
	Tess of the d'Urbervilles
	The Woodlanders
WALTER SCOTT	Ivanhoe
	Rob Roy
	Waverley
MARY SHELLEY	Frankenstein
	The Last Man
ROBERT LOUIS STEVENSON	Kidnapped and Catriona
	The Strange Case of Dr Jekyll and Mr Hyde and Weir of Hermiston
	Treasure Island
BRAM STOKER	Dracula
WILLIAM MAKEPEACE THACKERAY	Barry Lyndon
	Vanity Fair
OSCAR WILDE	Complete Shorter Fiction
	The Picture of Dorian Gray

Oriental Tales

WILLIAM BECKFORD   **Vathek**

JAMES BOSWELL   **Boswell's Life of Johnson**

FRANCES BURNEY   **Camilla**
Cecilia
Evelina
The Wanderer

LORD CHESTERFIELD   **Lord Chesterfield's Letters**

JOHN CLELAND   **Memoirs of a Woman of Pleasure**

DANIEL DEFOE   **Captain Singleton**
A Journal of the Plague Year
Memoirs of a Cavalier
Moll Flanders
Robinson Crusoe
Roxana

HENRY FIELDING   **Joseph Andrews and Shamela**
A Journey from This World to the Next and
    The Journal of a Voyage to Lisbon
Tom Jones
The Adventures of David Simple

WILLIAM GODWIN   **Caleb Williams**
St Leon

OLIVER GOLDSMITH   **The Vicar of Wakefield**

MARY HAYS   **Memoirs of Emma Courtney**

ELIZABETH HAYWOOD   **The History of Miss Betsy Thoughtless**

ELIZABETH INCHBALD   **A Simple Story**

SAMUEL JOHNSON   **The History of Rasselas**

CHARLOTTE LENNOX   **The Female Quixote**

MATTHEW LEWIS   **The Monk**

The Oxford World's Classics Website

www.worldsclassics.co.uk

- Information about new titles
- Explore the full range of Oxford World's Classics
- Links to other literary sites and the main OUP webpage
- Imaginative competitions, with bookish prizes
- Peruse *Compass*, the Oxford World's Classics magazine
- Articles by editors
- Extracts from Introductions
- A forum for discussion and feedback on the series
- Special information for teachers and lecturers

www.worldsclassics.co.uk

American Literature

British and Irish Literature

Children's Literature

Classics and Ancient Literature

Colonial Literature

Eastern Literature

European Literature

History

Medieval Literature

Oxford English Drama

Poetry

Philosophy

Politics

Religion

The Oxford Shakespeare

A complete list of Oxford Paperbacks, including Oxford World's Classics, OPUS, Past Masters, Oxford Authors, Oxford Shakespeare, Oxford Drama, and Oxford Paperback Reference, is available in the UK from the Academic Division Publicity Department, Oxford University Press, Great Clarendon Street, Oxford OX2 6DP.

In the USA, complete lists are available from the Paperbacks Marketing Manager, Oxford University Press, 198 Madison Avenue, New York, NY 10016.

Oxford Paperbacks are available from all good bookshops. In case of difficulty, customers in the UK can order direct from Oxford University Press Bookshop, Freepost, 116 High Street, Oxford OX1 4BR, enclosing full payment. Please add 10 per cent of published price for postage and packing.